REIMAGINING HISTORY IN CONT
THEATER, CINEMA, TELEVISION, STREAMING

# LEGENDA

LEGENDA is the Modern Humanities Research Association's book imprint for new research in the Humanities. Founded in 1995 by Malcolm Bowie and others within the University of Oxford, Legenda has always been a collaborative publishing enterprise, directly governed by scholars. The Modern Humanities Research Association (MHRA) joined this collaboration in 1998, became half-owner in 2004, in partnership with Maney Publishing and then Routledge, and has since 2016 been sole owner. Titles range from medieval texts to contemporary cinema and form a widely comparative view of the modern humanities, including works on Arabic, Catalan, English, French, German, Greek, Italian, Portuguese, Russian, Spanish, and Yiddish literature. Editorial boards and committees of more than 60 leading academic specialists work in collaboration with bodies such as the Society for French Studies, the British Comparative Literature Association and the Association of Hispanists of Great Britain & Ireland.

The MHRA encourages and promotes advanced study and research in the field of the modern humanities, especially modern European languages and literature, including English, and also cinema. It aims to break down the barriers between scholars working in different disciplines and to maintain the unity of humanistic scholarship. The Association fulfils this purpose through the publication of journals, bibliographies, monographs, critical editions, and the MHRA Style Guide, and by making grants in support of research. Membership is open to all who work in the Humanities, whether independent or in a University post, and the participation of younger colleagues entering the field is especially welcomed.

### ALSO PUBLISHED BY THE ASSOCIATION

*Critical Texts*
*Tudor and Stuart Translations* • *New Translations* • *European Translations*
*MHRA Library of Medieval Welsh Literature*

*MHRA Bibliographies*
*Publications of the Modern Humanities Research Association*

*The Annual Bibliography of English Language & Literature*
*Austrian Studies*
*Modern Language Review*
*Portuguese Studies*
*The Slavonic and East European Review*
*Working Papers in the Humanities*
*The Yearbook of English Studies*

www.mhra.org.uk
www.legendabooks.com

# VISUAL CULTURE

*Visual Culture* reflects the dynamism of a vibrant and fast-growing field which showcases the interdisciplinary nature of research in Modern Languages and the Humanities more generally. The series publishes cutting-edge monographs and edited collections on any aspect of global visual culture from the Middle Ages to the present day. In line with this expansive scope, areas of interest include photography, advertising, memorials, urban visual studies, installation and performance art, commercial art and design, museum and gallery studies, and text-image relations in a variety of media and contexts.

*Managing Editor*
Dr Graham Nelson, 41 Wellington Square, Oxford OX1 2JF, UK

www.legendabooks.com

# Reimagining History in Contemporary Spanish Media

*Theater, Cinema, Television, Streaming*

PAUL JULIAN SMITH

Modern Humanities Research Association

Visual Culture 1

2021

Published by Legenda
an imprint of the Modern Humanities Research Association
Salisbury House, Station Road, Cambridge CB1 2LA

ISBN 978-1-83954-040-0 (HB)
ISBN 978-1-83954-041-7 (PB)

First published 2021

Copy-Editor: Richard Correll

# CONTENTS

❖

# ACKNOWLEDGEMENTS

I would like to thank the faculty and students of the Comparative Literature Program in the CUNY Graduate Center for providing such a welcoming home for research. For this book, my warmest thanks go to Carolin Duttlinger, chair of the new series Studies in Visual Culture, with Graham Nelson, managing editor of Legenda. I'm most grateful for their kindness and efficiency and for the chance to publish with them. Richard Correll was the meticulous copyeditor. David Redondo, press manager at Atresmedia, kindly secured the permission for the handsome cover image from *Veneno*. Most of the material in these chapters was first presented in talks and conferences, in person or virtually, at events in Spain, the USA, and the UK. I am most grateful for the kind invitations, especially during the pandemic when intellectual community was at a premium. Beyond the invaluable authorities I have the pleasure of citing in this book (Concepción Cascajosa, Charo Lacalle, and Manuel Palacio), I am also grateful for the inspiration of pioneering Spanish television scholars working on the depiction of historical periods which are not my focus here (the Civil War, Francoism, and the Transition), such as Mar Chicharro Merayo, Carlota Coronado Ruiz, Elena Galán Fajardo, and José Carlos Rueda Laffond.

P.J.S, New York City, Summer 2021

# INTRODUCTION

## Reimagining History

The aim of this book is to explore the field of visual culture within contemporary Spanish studies in the specific case of the reimagining of past history for present audiences. To this end it introduces a new corpus of recent works in a number of audiovisual media (theater, cinema, television, and streaming of the last decade), works which have yet to receive scholarly attention. Intimately related to each other, they are submitted here to close reading. The book also stresses the intermediality of the visual by calling attention to connections between those media and others such as built environment or architecture, costume or dress, and fine art or painting.

*Reimagining History* is divided into three sections each of two chapters. The first section is on multimedia and its first chapter is 'The Javis: Theater, Cinema, Television, Streaming'. The young and versatile creators known as the Javis (professional and personal partners whose full names are Javier Ambrossi and Javier Calvo) have, over the last ten years, produced an ambitious body of work in theater, cinema, television, and streaming. Fiercely contemporary (described by the press as an unstoppable millennial phenomenon), the Javis are also surprisingly concerned with the audiovisual legacy of Spain, reimagining in defiantly queer fashion historical genres as varied as the religious dramas of the 1950s, the reality TV of the 1990s, and even the canonical theater of García Lorca.

The second chapter, 'Twenty-first-century Lorca: Historical Memory and Heritage in Theater, Cinema, and Television', further examines this reimagining of Lorca for the new millennium in three separate texts: an intimate theatrical performance, a feminist feature film, and an innovative TV drama. It argues that these diverse texts display three different strategies with queer or feminist implications for replaying the past and reengaging a contemporary public: displacement (where another historical figure is substituted for the poet), revisionism (where his original text is rewritten from a different, gendered perspective), and anachronism (where Lorca's own past time is juxtaposed with that of the viewer's present).

The second section treats TV period pieces, asking how television drama recreates a traumatic past in relation to its own history and to that of painting. This section is also transnational, drawing on material from the USA and Italy as well as Spain. The first chapter is called 'Two Televisual *Guernicas*: *Genius Picasso* and *El Ministerio del Tiempo*'. It examines the depiction of the figure of Picasso and more particularly his iconic *Guernica* in a hagiographic US bio-series and a more skeptical and ironic Spanish science fiction drama (the same series that had reimagined Lorca in my Chapter 2). These varied revisions of Picasso, like those of Lorca once more, are incompatible but not inexplicable, derived as they are from their different social and televisual contexts.

The fourth chapter, the only one not to deal with the present, is named for Spanish television's most prestigious and meticulous reproduction of the past, Mario Camus' reverent reimagining of Galdós. 'Fortunata Italiana? *Sceneggiato*, *Serie Clásica*, and TV Nation Formation' dives deep into television history and Europe's most loved and despised genre, the classic serial in its twin variants as literary adaption or bio-series once more. This chapter calls attention to Spanish television's little-known debt to Italy in this context and argues that the heritage period drama that remains influential today transcends its typically decorative *mise en scène*. Rather, the classic serial engages, in presentist style, with sociopolitical issues that are urgent to its contemporary audience, including the continuing engagement with a fascist past.

The third section intensifies the attention to gender. Keeping the focus on television drama, its first chapter treats two recent feminist-inspired series that are very different from one another. Its title is 'History Girls: *Arde Madrid* (Movistar+, 2018) and *La otra mirada* (TVE, 2018)'. The first series reimagines an American movie star's exile in the Francoist Madrid of the 1960s; the second recreates a progressive girls' school in the Seville of the 1920s. Calling attention once more to a carefully crafted production design (especially meticulous attention to period sets and costumes), these chapters argue once more that the past is not (or not just) the past; and that industrial and thematic aspects of these dramas are mutually reinforcing.

Moreover industrial context is vital here. *Arde Madrid* [Madrid is Burning] was made in the context of a new digital platform's quest for female creators, narratives, and audiences, while *La otra mirada* [A Different View] responded to an established public broadcaster's new search for openly feminist programming. To this end the latter series also recreates, scarcely veiled, contemporary scandals (such as a notorious gang rape) within the previously decorous setting of the heritage drama.

The second chapter of this third section treats Spain's unusually prominent contributions to the world's dominant streaming platform. In series initially targeted at Spanish women, local producers have attracted a global audience, especially in the USA, by appealing once more to their established competitive advantage in costume drama. Close attention is paid here to the social media footprint of such titles as evidence for audience response and to the American journalistic and fan reception of series that were nonetheless crafted for audiences in Spain and remain inseparable from that nation's history of production.

Finally the last chapter or 'Coda' ('Almodóvar and Aging') examines the director's most recent feature at the time of writing, *Dolor y gloria* [Pain and Glory] (2019). Set partly in an impoverished and traumatic past as recreated through the memory of a child, the film also explores the question of aging in relation to creative agency. Playing with autobiography or auto-fiction in the script as in the sets (even the paintings in the protagonist's apartment belong to the director himself), Almodóvar explores a fluid reimagining of his own and of Spain's past. And once more here visual and material culture (from a long lost portrait to a humble wooden darning egg) is indispensable.

The theme of aging is a private equivalent of the public historical narrative explored in the previous chapters. Apparently novel, it is in fact, as I show, prefigured in several of Almodóvar's earlier features from decades gone by. The long-lasting work of Spain's most respected audiovisual creator (his latest film, his *oeuvre* over some forty years) thus serves as a fitting conclusion to a book which explores the past and the present through the visual and the textual.

## Theater, Cinema, Television, Streaming

The main aim of the book is, as mentioned earlier, to present and analyze a new corpus of audiovisual texts from the decade of the teens in which the Spanish past is reexamined for the audiences of the present. What might seem surprising about that corpus, focused as it is on the twentieth century, is that the Civil War and Dictatorship, the most traumatic period and the one most studied by Hispanist scholars, is relatively absent.

Bio-series *Genius: Picasso* (2018) does recreate in bloodily convincing detail the bombing of Guernica; and, more obliquely, Alberto Conejero's play *La piedra oscura* [The Dark Stone] (2015) conjures up a vision of Lorca's last lover, a combatant in the War, just before his death. But the Javis, although clearly fascinated with Spanish history, make only sly, glancing references to the period. For example they refashion and lesbianize Francoist cinema's stalest genre, the religious drama, via their sole feature film and legitimate theater play, *La llamada* [Holy Camp] (2017). Movistar+'s streaming series *Arde Madrid* (2018) offers a darkly humorous take on the repressions of Spain in the 1960s, viewed by foreign celebrity Ava Gardner and her Spanish maid, a risibly incompetent spy put into place by the regime.

Conversely, the Javis tend to focus on the decade of the 1990s, ancient history for them and their young target audience, for example in a spoof episode of mockumentary comedy *Paquita Salas* from 2018 and in their more ambitious and extended bio-series *Veneno* (2020). Here the history of Spain and of its trans women is inextricable from the history of Spanish television and its celebration and exploitation of those same women.

Several works that I examine here are set in the so-called 'happy 1920s'. The bureaucrats of the Ministry of Time encounter Lorca, Buñuel, and Dalí during their period of joyful creative ferment at the Residencia de Estudiantes [Students Residence Hall] in Madrid. *La otra mirada*, also from TVE, takes place in a progressive high school in Seville in the same decade (in one episode, the feminist-inclined staff and students receive a visit from the real-life pioneer of girls' education, María de Maeztú). And Netflix's globally successful *Las chicas del cable* [Cable Girls] (2017–20) places its ambitious young women in the modernizing Madrid of the same pre-Civil War period. While the 'classic series' of the 1970s make some implicit reference to the Francoist era through their warnings on the violent divisions of the nineteenth century, their aim is more to seek out progressive icons of the past (Pérez Galdós,

Lorca once more) in order to educate Spanish audiences on their new rights and responsibilities in the Transition to democracy.

The key intertext here is painting. *La otra mirada*'s credits show a paintbrush reimagining the series' new women in new artistic styles. And in *El Ministerio del Tiempo*, *Guernica*'s arrival in Spain (wrongly but significantly called at the time its 'return') is said to serve as the symbolic resolution of past conflict. But architecture and costume also bear more or less mute witness to historical process in my corpus. Authentic locations such as the Residencia de Estudiantes add gravity and glamor to the reimagining of Lorca and Buñuel; the lavish studio recreation of central Madrid in *Fortunata y Jacinta* (1980) testifies to the young democracy's expert appeal to a progressive past; and Netflix's 'girls' work in a new skyscraper on Madrid's Gran Vía based on the celebrated real-life Telefónica building. It is the architectural icon of a hopeful modernity that would be betrayed by the War that is shown in the series' last season.

As I note in Chapter 6, all three of the Netflix series I treat reference this historic avenue in the capital, a location unlikely to be familiar to foreign audiences. And even the globalizing and consciously contemporary thriller *La casa de papel* [Money Heist] (2017–21) relies on a historic built environment well known to *madrileños*, even when those authentic locations are misidentified within the show itself. They include the Plaza de Callao (where millions of euros are made to rain from the skies), the classically inspired Mint and Bank of Spain, and the massive and forbidding Nuevos Ministerios [New Ministries] complex, completed in the early years of the Dictatorship.

Beyond architecture, *Reimagining History* seeks also to take seriously another key feature of art design: costume or wardrobe. The Javis are as meticulous in recreating 1990s fashions as they are in reproducing period media technology (primitive cellphones and Walkmans) and La Veneno's transition is charted by her changing wardrobe. The three protagonists of the first season of *El Ministerio del Tiempo* (2015) are handily distinguished by their costumes, from the sixteenth, nineteenth, and twenty-first centuries, respectively. Lorca and Picasso are unapologetically dandyish in their series; while the girls of *La otra mirada* obsess over Parisian trends (their feminist teachers tell them that they should wear makeup to please only themselves and not boys). And of course the nineteenth-century Jacinta is constrained as much by her tight corsets and voluminous skirts as she is by the bourgeois ideology which, initially at least, confines her to the role of angel of the hearth even as she is based (like Netflix's 'girls' some forty years later) in the heart of Madrid.

Beyond an objective index of time, production design also serves as a subjective testimony to character. Ava Gardner's décolletage is the frankly sensual riposte of a free-living American to strait-laced Francoist women, as is her brightly modern home, all glass and chrome, a festive beacon in the dark days of the Dictatorship. Or again, Almodóvar's child protagonist Salvador is raised in a cave, proof of the desperate poverty of his post-War family. But the hushed luxury of the adult Salvador's home in the present time, an apartment densely hung with paintings, is if anything more oppressive than the whitewashed cave, reminiscent as it is of a museum or even a mausoleum. The production design is here the image of an aging man's depression, even as it documents the visual pleasures of a life lived for art.

With recent changes in distribution and exhibition, the production values of free-to-air television and of streaming services rival those once so jealously monopolized by the cinema to which Almodóvar remains loyal. As we shall see, it is symptomatic that in 2020 a huge billboard promoting the Javis' series *Veneno* was hung over the Gran Vía, which remains the site of some of Madrid's most glamorous picture palaces. And, in spite of pandemic restrictions, the first two episodes of the series broke attendance records when screened at those same historic movie theaters. In reimagining the past, then, current Spanish cinema, television, and streaming have converged to make the single object of study which I explore here.

To conclude, a note on secondary sources which remain rare for my recent primary texts. In Chapter 4, uniquely, I cite at length academic authorities, especially Manuel Palacio for the Spanish *serie clásica* and Milly Buonanno for the *sceneggiato*, its Italian equivalent. Here I am treating works from an earlier period that have received a full measure of specialist commentary. One rare expert scholarly contributor on very current material, who also practices public writing, is Palacio's colleague, Concepción Cascajosa Virino, whom I cite on *Veneno*. For the chapters on the recent audiovisual works, my appeal to academic sources is of necessity more oblique (for example I cite earlier audiovisual reimaginings of Lorca in Chapter 2 or treatments of Guernica in disciplines other than media or Hispanic studies in Chapter 3). Elsewhere I have relied on the expert commentary of the trade press, in the US *The Hollywood Reporter* and *Variety* (where John Hopewell remains the master of coverage on Spanish-language film and TV); and in Spain the exhaustive specialist website Formulatv.com.

As for the general press, in a major shift that no doubt mirrors the changing attitudes of its readers, Spain's *El País* is now less hostile to television than it long was and offers some sympathetic commentary on innovative titles such as *Arde Madrid*. In Chapter 6, which focuses on American reception of Spanish Netflix titles, I appeal to the *New York Times* as arbiter of elegance for its busy upscale readership, which the daily assumes has little time to surf the new tide of streaming services. This chapter is also the one in which I examine most closely social media. Here Twitter is taken as evidence for English-speaking reception of Spanish series. The key case study here is period romance *Las chicas del cable*, in which American viewers made such a lengthy and emotional investment of time and feeling.

Finally I trust that this book, the first full-length study of its kind, will stimulate further specialist study of a corpus that it seeks to make more visible to readers. Just so does that corpus seek to reimagine the past more clearly and vividly for its faithful fans.

## References: Audiovisual

*Arde Madrid*. 2018. (Andy Joke/Movistar+)
*casa de papel, La*. 2017–present. (Atresmedia/Netflix)
*chicas del cable, Las*. 2017–20. (Bambú/Netflix)

*Dolor y gloria.* 2019. Dir. by Pedro Almodóvar (El Deseo)
*Fortunata y Jacinta.* 1980. Dir. by Mario Camus (RTVE/TéléFrance)
*Genius: Picasso.* 2018. (EUE/Sokolow/National Geographic)
*llamada, La.* 2017. Dir. by Javier Ambrossi and Javier Calvo (Apache Films)
*Ministerio del Tiempo, El.* 2015–20. (Cliffhanger/RTVE)
*otra mirada, La.* 2018–19. (Boomerang/RTVE)
*Paquita Salas.* 2016–present. (Flooxer/Neox/Netflix)
*Veneno.* 2020. (Atresmedia Studios/HBO Max)

# PART I

# Multimedia

# CHAPTER 1

# The Javis:
# Theater, Cinema, Television, Streaming

### From *La llamada* [Holy Camp] to *Paquita Salas*, Season 1

It is autumn 2017 in Madrid and, five weeks after its release, an unlikely fiction feature from two first-time directors is still playing on twenty screens. In candy-colored musical *La llamada* (literally 'The Call', official English title 'Holy Camp!'), a teenage girl and would-be singing star named María, on vacation in a rural Catholic summer camp, receives visitations from God. Surprisingly, he takes the form of a middle-aged man wearing a rhinestone-studded tuxedo who serenades her with Whitney Houston numbers.

Although star Macarena García previously took the title role in Pablo Berger's silent, monochrome art movie *Blancanieves* [Snow White] (2012), she appears on *La llamada*'s gaudy poster dressed in the camp uniform of canary yellow T-shirt and grass-green short shorts. It is an image that would seem to confirm the impression that this is just a kitsch comedy. And reaction from veteran cinephile journal *Cinemanía* was dismissive. Reviewer Yago García enumerates the film's supposed faults: its musical numbers are deliberately 'clumsy', its invocation of the 'stalest' genre of Francoism (films about priests and nuns) is 'fake', and its aspiration to combine mysticism with reggaeton 'repellent' (García 2017).

The language is reminiscent of attacks by established critics on Pedro Almodóvar thirty years before, most especially their dismissal of his early *Entre tinieblas* [Dark Habits] (1983), in which a nightclub chanteuse seeks shelter in a convent run by a lesbian Mother Superior. What such criticism of *La llamada* misses, as again in the case of Almodóvar so long ago, is the emergence of a new youthful sensibility and a new gay auteurism. In this case it is that of young writer-directors Javier Ambrossi (born 1984) and Javier Calvo (born 1991), who are universally known as celebrities in Spain by the diminutive of their shared first name as 'los Javis'. The back story to their first feature film, whose success so mystifies the established film press, is one of the couple's canny and creative appeal to the multiple media of theater, television, and streaming.

As actors, the two men shared credits on television, with Calvo best known as a much-loved gay teen on the controversial high school drama *Física o química* [Physics or Chemistry] (Antena 3, 2008–11). Typecast and unemployed after the series ended, the couple were reduced to tending bar. Between serving cocktails,

FIG. 1.1. On location for *La llamada* from left: María (Macarena García),
co-director Javier Calvo, Susana (Anna Castillo), novice Milagros (Belén Cuesta),
Sister Bernarda (Gracia Olayo), co-director Javier Ambrossi

the Javis devised the first small-scale version of *La llamada* which was staged in the lobby of the jewel box-like Lara Theater in fashionable Malasaña, Madrid's version of young, trendy Williamsburg. It is a theater with multiple Almodóvar associations: its gorgeous stage curtain was shown in the last shot of *Todo sobre mi madre* [All About My Mother] (1999) and the first of *Hable con ella* [Talk to Her] (2002); and Carmen Maura had stalked its stage and Antonio Banderas lurked in its ornate lobby in *La ley del deseo* [The Law of Desire] (1987) (see Sánchez Castrejón 2017). After graduating to the main stage of the theater, *La llamada* had run in 2017, when the film version was released, for four years to a total audience of some three hundred thousand. There was also a national tour of Spain and a Mexican version.

At a sold-out performance in the Lara Theater also in 2017 I was able to confirm the continuing devotion of the cult crowd to a piece that is unusually immersive. Much of the action takes place in the aisle amongst the faithful audience; and God descends, belting out ballads, down a silver staircase from the mezzanine to the orchestra. While the play features some broad humor in the contrast between the (initially) sheltered Sisters and the (also initially) pill-popping, electro-dancing kids, it also displays a transparent affection for all the characters, one in which the show's devoted fans clearly share.

The Javis' next project as writer-directors was a sitcom of just five thirty-minute episodes made for network Antena 3's OTT video player Flooxer, but picked up from its second season by Netflix (it had begun yet more modestly as a series of ten-second skits on Instagram). *Paquita Salas* (2017–), prosaically named for its protagonist, is a prize-winning single-camera comedy about a failing fifty-year-

FIG. 1.2. Brays Efe as Paquita Salas in the Javis' comedy series of the same name

old showbiz agent, reminiscent of Anglo-American mockumentaries such as *The Office* (BBC, 2001–03; NBC, 2005–13). The project is more original in Spain than it would be in the UK or US, however, in that in Spanish broadcast television there is no tradition of short-form sitcom, as local production consists of series made up of seventy-minute episodes which combine elements of drama and comedy.

What is truly striking in *Paquita Salas* is that the mature female protagonist is here played by a much younger man (Brays Efe), but without the slightest trace of camp. Indeed the directors insisted that the humor be as realist as possible. Thus real-life Spanish stars, major and minor, play themselves in the show, which was shot in part guerrilla-style on location on city streets. Even the Javis themselves, who do not appear on screen, serve as butts of the show's metacomedy: looking at a photo of a young actor, Paquita remarks complacently that it is always a career mistake to take on gay roles in Spain, especially when you are actually gay. The head shot she shows the camera is of Javier Calvo himself.

Similarly, throughout the first episode, Paquita desperately tries to contact her big star, Macarena García (in real life the winner of a Best Actress Goya, or Spanish Oscar), oblivious to the fact that García has already dumped her for a better agent in an email missed by Paquita's flustered secretary Magüi ('What's a spam file?'). In the final moving scene, shot at the real-life Valladolid Film Festival, the publicly humiliated Paquita waves goodbye to her prized discovery ('I made her out of nothing!') having lovingly costumed her in the dress she wears on the red carpet. In a typically ambivalent detail, Paquita has failed to do up her ex-star's zipper, proof perhaps of the kind of mistake for which her client abandoned her.

Subsequent episodes develop this queasy comedy of embarrassment. In the second episode Paquita signs up a homely fat girl who has played the maid in a production of Ibsen at an acting school (Paquita, typically, thinks 'Hedda Gabler' is the name of the play's author). In the third, she returns to her tiny home town to visit her TV-addict mother and a former aspiring actor, Clara, whose career she has ruined by encouraging her to fake success in Hollywood. Paquita offers viewers a nostalgic tour of the village, including the site of her first kiss: 'Francisco Franco Square', still named for the long-dead dictator (Spain was at the very time debating its charged heritage of historic monuments). In the fourth episode, Paquita is reduced to sleeping with her elderly ex-husband, a producer, in order to obtain an audition for her new charge. And in the fifth, against all the odds, the overweight, talent-free new signing not only gains the lead role in a controversial drama called 'Eat Shit' but wins a Best Actress Goya award. Like Macarena before her, she will swiftly dump the agent who discovered her.

But in spite of the cruelties they inflict on them, the Javis are always sympathetic to their flawed, failing characters. The last episode shows the now greedy and slovenly Paquita, who, in the words of one of the series' assured original songs has swapped 'estrellas' [stars] for 'mozzarella' (on pizza), dressed up to the nines in fur coat and big hair. Triumphantly she signs a new female actor who currently works behind a bar, just as the series' real-life directors once did. This time she tells her with hard-won experience: 'I'll make you a star. And then you will leave me'.

Belén, the new signing, is played by Anna Castillo, another real-life Goya winner for an auteur film, this time Icíar Bollaín's earnest environmental drama *El olivo* [The Olive Tree] (2016). Castillo is also the co-star of both stage and screen versions of *La llamada*. Meanwhile, Macarena García is not just Castillo's partner in the musical but also the real-life sister of one of the Javis, Javier Ambrossi. If we return to the feature film, then, this sense of an intricately linked family of actors crossing over from television to cinema comes through in the warmth and tenderness with which the crazy, kitsch material is treated.

Learning perhaps from their experience on mockumentary *Paquita*, the Javis opt as novice film directors for authentic locations that cinematically transform their theatrical original. The summer camp is now convincingly set in a real forest and is staffed by additional characters (a love-sick cook, an amorous zip line engineer) that do not appear in the stripped-down stage version. Celestial digital effects and fluid camerawork make God's sequined apparitions yet more impressive. Most importantly the cast and crew employ close-ups to lead us emotionally through the film's two parallel journeys: one girl's unexpected discovery of love for God and another's equally surprising passion for a young nun. When I saw the stage version the audience applauded wildly when the unlikely lesbian couple shared a first kiss.

It is here that the Javis make their special contribution to Spanish cultural and film history. In Almodóvar's *Entre tinieblas*, to which *La llamada* bears a passing resemblance, the love between younger singer and older nun was tragically unrequited. In *La llamada*, on the other hand, the affair is physical. The Javis both cheerfully reference the erotic visions of a tradition of Spanish mysticism that stretches back to St Teresa of Ávila and joyfully lesbianize the Francoist priest and nun films which, as *Cinemanía* wrote, make up the 'stalest' of the regime's cinematic genres. And even the unsympathetic *Cinemanía* admitted that *La llamada* chooses not to attack easy religious targets and enjoys 'the luxury of dispensing with irony'. It is this appeal to genuine feeling within an artificial setting (in theater, TV, and film) that makes Calvo and Ambrossi's work so fresh and attractive to wide audiences. National newspaper of record *El País* called the Javis 'an unstoppable millennial revolution' (Mirate 2017).

The couple's motto, tattooed on their forearms and used as the title of one of *La llamada*'s original songs, is 'Lo hacemos y ya veremos' [rough translation: Just do it]. Perhaps this was why one of the Javis spontaneously proposed marriage to the other at the world premiere of their film at the San Sebastián International Film Festival, Spain's most important. But the two writer-directors have clearly thought long and hard about their projects. And their success was rewarded, also in fall 2017, by a unlikely starring role on mainstream television's biggest hit: as twin coaches on *Operación Triunfo* [Operation Triumph] (TVE, 2001–), Spain's equivalent of *American Idol* (Fox, 2002–). It is a responsibility that they have taken on with a characteristic mix of humor and earnestness manifest both on the inescapable TV show itself and in the couple's zealously tended Twitter feeds (although one of them would later quit social media).

But the Javis not only created a remarkably intelligent and enjoyable body of work in a short period; they also pioneered a new model of auteurship for popular film, in Spain and perhaps elsewhere, by combining the heritage media of theater, feature film, and free-to-air television with the new media of Instagram and OTT streaming. It is a remarkable achievement in a country where young audiences are notoriously hostile to locally produced cinema, most especially the serious auteur films for which, ironically enough, the two stars of the Javis' musical comedy won their Best Actress accolades.

Meanwhile, as we shall see, the second season of *Paquita Salas*, promoted by a short in which the accident-prone agent comes to America, would stream on Netflix in 2018. And *La llamada*, the little film that could, was nominated in Spain for no fewer than five Goya awards. Although the conservative Academy spurned the Javis in the category of 'Best New Directors', their first (and to date only) film won for 'Best Song' and 'Best Supporting Actress', an accolade shared by young lovers Anna Castillo and Belén Cuesta, who also plays the bumbling secretary Magüi in *Paquita Salas*.

## *Paquita Salas*, Seasons 2 and 3

After their hard-won but precocious successes in various media in 2017, the Javis found themselves in a quandary: how to expand a brand built on youth and novelty into a mature franchise with staying power. And in the second and third seasons of *Paquita Salas*, a series whose future was now safely secured by Netflix, the showrunners extended their famously contemporary creations, paradoxically enough, by turning or returning more than ever to the past, to a visual heritage which constitutes a precious legacy of personal memory for characters and creators alike. It is telling that when Paquita returns to the stifling village where she was raised, she should say with some solemnity: 'It is here that I learned to love television'.

In recent seasons of the show, that treasured past is mediated by period visualizing technology or embodied in treasured objects of material culture (dog-eared snapshots, grainy video cassettes, and boxy Sony Walkmans), even as it is ironized by willful and playful anachronism. Memories of a folkloric past (most especially as depicted by the theater of Federico García Lorca) are also juxtaposed with the most urgent of modern issues, such as the #MeToo movement and transgender casting. These are both potentially controversial topics for a show whose female protagonist is played by a cisgender male actor. In #MeToo plotlines Paquita's client Belén will be humiliated both as an aspiring actor, reduced to playing a murder victim in a tacky procedural show, and as an aspiring screenwriter, belittled in a pitch meeting by patronizing male executives. Meanwhile in a transgender plotline on a second visit to her home village, Paquita will bond with a trans girl who has Downs Syndrome and defend her from her abusive father.

Television history (or rather history on television) is explored in an ingenious episode 2.3. Here Paquita helps long-term client Lidia San José (a modestly successful real-life actor playing a version of herself) land a role on *El secreto de Puente Viejo* [The Secret of Puente Viejo] (Antena 3, 2011–). This is one of the low-status daytime period soaps, scorned by the critics, that have recently taken the place of once prestigious classic serials on Spanish network schedules. Shot on the costume drama's actual set with its real cast, the episode is a favorite of the Javis, who call it 'conceptual'. Just as the Javis, as creators, turn to a show set in the past to explore the present, so here their character Lidia, beset by stage fright, will be cured by returning to and working through a childhood trauma she had suffered in another TV studio. Typically for *Paquita Salas*, Lidia appeals once more to the institution of television itself, as embodied by a kindly cast member from long ago (veteran thespian Antonio Resines, an established star in Spain), who will solve her problem.

But the most historically engaged episode of this season is its finale. Number 2.5 is titled 'Punto de partida' [The Starting Point] after a song that is unusually melodramatic even by the standards of its singer, the diva Rocío Jurado. Here Paquita is forced to quit her office after a professional failure. Packing up her things in this intensely charged place of memory, she comes across an old photo of herself and secretary Magüi, eternal female friends, and a Sony Walkman complete with a cassette that plays British boy band Take That's nostalgic ballad 'Back for Good'.

As Paquita listens and looks with complicity directly into the camera, the episode transitions to a digital recreation of the blurry video format of 1994, with its boxy academy ratio and horizontal interference bars. We are next treated to faux credits for a series also called *Paquita Salas*: in lurid color, the featured cast, now made up and costumed as their younger selves, grin complacently into the camera. And in a touch of willful anachronism and of playful satire on the Javis' powerful new distributor, we are told that this show, supposedly set and shot twenty five years ago, is 'A Series by Netflix'.

Paquita's current adult clients are shown in this episode as children at the hopeful opening of her then new office. And there is also a cameo by established movie star Paz Vega, appearing here in the role of a humble waitress who, as her younger self, speaks with the native Andalusian accent that she would later abandon. Period references in this special 'conceptual' episode are typically to television shows and executives of the time (family dramedy *Médico de familia* [Family Doctor] (Telecinco, 1995–99); pioneer showrunner Daniel Écija), but also self-reflexively to *Paquita Salas* itself. A minor drama over a missing fax ('The fax!' 'What fax?') here replays or prefigures a crisis over a mislaid email in the very first episode of the first season ('The email!' 'What email?'). The close attention to communication technology is once more typical of the Javis.

Likewise an oversized photo portrait of Paquita's star client hangs once more on the office wall. Where previously (latterly) it had been of Macarena García, now (in the distant '90s) it is of Miriam Díaz Aroca. Currently somewhat forgotten, Díaz Aroca is presented here as an imperious star of the '90s proud to have been paid '1000 pesetas' (a risible sum) more than her fellow female protagonists in the Oscar-winning costume drama *Belle époque* (Fernando Trueba, 1992). Unspoken, but inevitable here, is an implied contrast with the success of one of Díaz Aroca's companions in the cast of that film: unlike the faded Díaz Aroca, Penélope Cruz is now a global superstar.

This somewhat cruel comedy of embarrassment (in which real-life minor celebrities prove surprisingly willing to participate) is contrasted with moments of the heartfelt sentiment in which the Javis also specialize: Paquita will pass on an important dinner with an executive and star client (Díaz Aroca once more) to celebrate the solitary birthday of her lonely child client Lidia (there is just one improvised candle on the tiny cake). And in a final montage sequence which takes place back in the present once more and is set to the titular number by Rocío Jurado playing at full, histrionic length, Paquita, exiled from her office, walks the mean streets of Madrid at night. She is carrying a pathetic cardboard box that contains 'all her life', including that treasured photo and Walkman. As she paces through the city, she passes multiple girls in doorways, all reading aloud from scripts for the auditions that they hope will serve as their 'point of departure' and make them a star. As if by magic, the present-day celebrity Paz Vega also returns at the end of the episode, to tell a struggling waitress that she (like the Javis) once worked in a bar herself.

But it is in the twin, linked episodes of the finale to the third season (3.5 'Bailes regionales' [Regional Dances] and 3.6 'Hasta Navarrete II' [Back to Navarrete II]) that the Javis create the most moving references to the Spanish cultural legacy and the most tenderly self-mocking account of their own trajectory to date. The former episode, in which Paquita returns to her village for her mother's funeral, was first titled 'La casa de Paquita Salas' [The House of Paquita Salas] as a transparent homage to Lorca's last play *La casa de Bernarda Alba* [The House of Bernarda Alba] (1936), a rare theater classic cast only with women (we remember that the initially severe Mother Superior in *La llamada* was also called Bernarda).

In an unpublished article Daniel Valtueña (2020) has traced what he calls 'a homosexual genealogy' that stretches here from Lorca to the Javis via Almodóvar's *Volver* (2006), another rural tragedy. Valtueña notes the Javis' occasional explicit references to their hallowed predecessors, but does not seek naively to identify particular moments of influence in their series. Rather he calls attention to general themes re-explored by the three (or four) artists: maternity, liberty, sexual desire, the questioning of patriarchy, and the subversion of image repertoires traditionally associated with Spanishness. Taking my own point of departure from this last theme or strategy, I will limit myself here to the episodes' exploration of the three temporal spheres of the past, the present, and the anachronistic coexistence of the two.

The episode title itself suggests an echo of Francoist state-sponsored folklore, as regional dances and their picturesque costumes were a safe and reassuring staple of popular culture during the Dictatorship. Here the reference to the past is via the *jota*, a dance genre that is common in its regional variations across northern Spain but unlike flamenco, say, is little known abroad. A moving backstory associated with this dance surfaces in an important subplot. Memories of the *jota* will enable the stony Paquita, who refuses to acknowledge her mother's sudden death and even works and eats off the coffin, finally to reconnect with her feelings. Sitting with a childhood friend in the patio of her mother's modest house, Paquita recounts how she was humiliatingly thrown out of dance classes as a child for being overweight, but still learned the steps by secretly watching through the window (shades of the maternal melodrama *Stella Dallas* [King Vidor] (1937) here). Paquita, her adult friend, and the transgender girl (who is dressed for the local fiesta in regional costume) will now dance a joyful *jota* together, the image of an ancient tradition's persistence into an uncertain and troubling present.

This episode's *mise en scène* is, exceptionally in what is a very urban series, that of the rural village, with its annual fiesta and homely homes decorated by crucifixes and devotional images, its women in black mourning garb weeping at a wake. This image repertoire is all knowingly reminiscent of Lorca's Andalusia, even though Paquita's Navarrete is situated by the series in the northern region of La Rioja. At one point Paquita even directly echoes the matriarch Bernarda Alba, shouting 'Silence!' at her unruly female companions. The Lorcan theme of deadly public shame also recurs. But here the enforcers of female modesty are not the inquisitive neighbors of the immediate village but the intrusive social and mainstream media of the whole nation. Belinda Washington, a real-life actor who is, along with Lidia, Paquita's most loyal client, is hounded here because of a sex tape she has mistakenly unleashed on the internet. And Clara, the actor whose career Paquita helped to destroy and subsequently sent into hiding, is also discovered in cloistered Navarrete by the rabid press who set siege to the house.

The community of five female friends trapped inside that house (compare Lorca's five sisters, also unable to exit the family home) are conflictive but finally supportive. In the last sequence, Paquita and her companions, all dignified for once, bravely face down the cameras and carry the mother's coffin down the narrow village street. Ex-client Clara, meanwhile, opens up the window blinds and lets light flood into the once gloomy rooms, a sensual pleasure that Lorca's mourning daughters were unable to enjoy.

Yet the key technique here is not the slavish imitation of the past but rather a creative and anachronistic crosscutting. It is telling that as Paquita happily dances the *jota* with her village friend and the child, the soundtrack we hear is not the traditional folk music to which they would normally dance but an incongruous pop rock number. The episode has established that this is being played by a musical group in another location, the village bar to which Paquita's friends have snuck out to celebrate the local fiesta. There is thus a blurring of time periods, as there is of soundtrack, via clashing modes of song, dance, and festivity.

Oddly the related and final episode (3.6), the most recent available at the time of writing, is the one titled 'Hasta Navarrete II', even though it takes place back in Madrid once more. It is here that Belén pitches a script to patronizing male executives, in a clear reference to the indignities of women in the movie industry highlighted by #MeToo. Her script is based on the life of Clara, who disappeared in distress to Navarrete after feigning a glamorous Hollywood career (the men say that 'no one' can identify with such a story). Meanwhile a tacky parody pop video in praise of masturbation from Belinda, who has learned to monetize her shame, marks the series' return to cheerfully coarse humor after the melancholic drama of the previous episode.

At a reunion with her former secretary Magüi, now the producer of biopic for which Belén has indeed managed to find funding, Paquita learns that she herself is also a key figure in the future film. She is dismayed by this betrayal of trust until she realizes that she is being played by Juan Echanove, a celebrated actor. When the two meet he is extravagantly flattering to her as the revered source of his performance, although rudely dismissive of his junior colleagues on set (we have seen already that real-life stars on the show are artfully self-deprecating). Yet how, Paquita wonders (wonders Brays Efe, the man playing Paquita), is it possible in the current climate that Paquita can be played by a man? The irony is yet more evident when we remember that Paquita's client Lidia had been vilified on social media, also in the third season, for planning to take on the role of a transgender man herself.

A lengthy rehearsal sequence for the fake film within the series replays comic scenes from all three seasons, which are now themselves part of Spanish TV history, at least for the Javis' attentive audience. Paquita, soon to be the protagonist of a major motion picture, is clearly flattered to be the object of media attention. But she is not the only one to enjoy this dramatic revisualization, as faithful fans of the series are also gratified by their own remembrance of past plot points in this final episode.

In a radical shift of tone once more, the actor playing Clara delivers a lengthy, tearful monologue straight to camera telling her hapless and hopeless tale of professional deception. She recounts how her use of crudely photoshopped images (her face on Orlando Bloom's body) and easily debunked lies (a recurring role on a famous US sitcom, an invitation to the Oscars) had led her to disappear in shame, abandoning her one true love: the acting career for which she had sacrificed so much. The sad (funny?) irony here she is that this actor is played, perfectly, by Anna Allen, the real-life origin for the series' 'Clara' plotline. Allen was tempted out of her seclusion by the kindly Javis. This sequence is, as Concepción Cascajosa notes (2020), a dizzying *mise en abyme*.

The directors' affection for actors and for victims (and for actors who are victims) is shown by their offering Allen a second chance after past disgrace, a gesture that is movingly clear here. And in real life, after this touching cameo Anna Allen would land a recurring role on *Cuéntame cómo pasó* [Tell Me How It Happened] (RTVE, 2001–), TVE's most prestigious and durable period drama. In a further coincidence, this series was also home for no less than twelve years to the Juan Echanove who was cast by the Javis as Paquita on the big screen (although they had previously offered the role to Antonio Banderas). On being fired from *Cuéntame* in real life, Echanove had shown public signs of the explosive bad temper the Javis lend his character in their fiction (Redacción Barcelona 2017).

We cut in this final episode to the premiere, where the (fictional) film is a huge hit. Afterwards even art-house director Julio Medem, playing himself of course, expresses an interest in collaborating with the team; and the once humiliated Belinda is mobbed by equally mature fans who, incongruously, sing along to her crude hymn to self-pleasuring 'Cinco deditos' [Five Little Fingers].

The last shot of the last season is an image of continuing female friendship, as all of Paquita's companions celebrate together, just as they had served more solemnly as pallbearers at her mother's funeral in the previous episode. And the tune that plays over the final credits is by El Niño de Elche. Like the Javis he is a radical re-interpreter of Spanish tradition for a modern era, in this case flamenco. In another subtly coded reference that goes further to construct a continuing TV genealogy, El Niño's gentle, sensual song is called 'Un veneno' [A Poison]. Its name points forward to the subject of the Javis' next project, Cristina Ortiz 'La Veneno', who was a mainstay of Spanish television in the Javis' favorite decade of the 1990s.

### *Veneno*: Production and Consumption

On 5 July 2019 I attended a sold-out live event by the Javis in Madrid which was intended to promote the third season of *Paquita Salas* and to connect with television professionals and fans alike. It was sponsored by specialist website 'Fuera de Series', a punning name which coincides with the Javis' exceptionalism (the phrase 'fuera de serie' in the singular means 'mold breaking') and their ironic take on the TV medium (the 'series' in the plural which had by now become the focus of a national conversation on the audiovisual arts).

Part of a season of talks billed as 'Entre bambalinas' [Backstage], the event's site was also significant. It was held in a room at the Telefónica building in the Gran Vía, the main location, lightly fictionalized, of Netflix's then current period drama *Las chicas del cable* [Cable Girls] (2017–20). As Madrid's first skyscraper, originally built to house a brand-new telegraph and telephony facility, and more recently the longtime host of both a gallery of contemporary art and a museum of historic communication technology, the Telefónica combines the qualities also characteristic of the Javis: modernity, tradition, and the self-conscious awareness of multiple media.

It was at this event that the Javis spoke of their pride in the 'conceptual episodes' of the second season such as the *El secreto de Puente Viejo* and 1990s installments; and of Lorca's *La casa de Bernarda Alba* as the inspiration for the fifth episode of the third season. Questioned by the fashionable host (he wore a kilt), they went on to offer valuable evidence for their production process at this stage in their career. Now, they claimed, the 'pressure' on them had been relieved by Netflix, even as they faced higher expectations after their initial success. Key here is their work with the cast. The aim, they said, was to make each actor comfortable and use her distinct sensibility.

For example, Belinda Washington (who is given the most farcical plotline in the third season, with her crude sex tape) aims nonetheless for naturalism or serious drama, while all around her the rest of the cast go for humor. Meanwhile the performance of Noemí (a foul-mouthed fan favorite who is promoted, implausibly, from hairdresser to head of press in Paquita's agency) employs a combination of scripting and improvisation. Here there was lengthy preparation with experienced actor Yolanda Ramos, in which she even made changes to the dialogue before the shoot (meticulously scripted, *Paquita Salas* only appears to be improvised).

Conversely Terelu Campos, who is not an actor but a famous, even notorious, presenter of real-life TV talk, memorized her lines just as they were written. In a video segment at the talk, she testified that the Javis 'respect' everyone who appears on the show. This is in spite of the fact that her own appearance as a tyrannical fashion house boss might appear to be a prime example of stunt casting, as the Spanish audience has long been familiar with her very different real-life role on the celebrity gossip shows known as 'tertulias' [get-togethers]. The evidence from within the fictional world, then, of the creators' affection for their flawed characters, was reinforced here by the account of their working methods with talented but vulnerable actors in the real, professional world.

The transgender theme of the third season is another case in point. This plotline, the Javis said, was not a response to the rare critics or activists who had decried the casting of a cisgender gay man, Bryce Efe, as Paquita. Rather the Javis required the space of a new full season that was long enough to explore the subject in depth (in addition to the child *jota* dancer, the third season also features a transwoman assistant). Javier Calvo stated to applause that trans actors should now at the very least be cast in trans parts, although ideally they should be seen in general roles too.

With such newly serious ambitions, the show, then, is no longer a parody but rather boasts 'three-dimensional characters' (once more this could be seen an in joke or ironic reference to the show itself: Paquita repeatedly mentions her quest for a versatile '3D actress' who can save the agency). The Javis' characters are now so convincing that they claimed that journalists had called them asking to interview Paquita, without being aware that she was fictional. Conversely Javier Calvo claimed at another point that 'people understand reality best through fiction'.

The combination of an attention to urgent contemporary themes with the archeology of sometimes obscure TV history is seen in the precedents mentioned for Paquita at the event. The Fuera de Series presenter suggested meta-TV moments which ranged from the recent American cable comedy *The Comeback* (HBO, 2005–14), whose 'uncomfortableness' stemmed from the protagonist being played by a veteran of hallowed sitcom *Friends* (NBC, 1994–2004) who had now lost her celebrity vehicle, to the Spanish *Chicas de hoy en día* [Girls of Today] (RTVE, 1991–92), a little-known dramedy on two struggling female actors in Madrid. Bryce Efe, who participated in the event on video, cited both the American network show *Smash* (NBC, 2012–13) (on the mounting of a fake Broadway musical) and French Netflix's *Dix pour cent* [Call My Agent] (2015–20) (with its queasy cameos by famous film stars, riffing on their public personas).

The international references were telling. When asked on feedback from abroad, the Javis replied that *Paquita* was popular as far away as Korea. The creators had thus come to understand that the series can be understood even by international audiences who are ignorant of its constant Spanish references. Their challenge as directors was to go beyond this now familiar faux documentary to fully fledged drama; and to expand the episode length from twenty to fifty minutes. Their next project was to be a biographical series on the tragic trans TV star of the 1990s known as La Veneno, then still at the research stage.

After its two opening episodes were completed in 2020 a massive billboard for *Veneno*, featuring the most glamorous of the three trans actors who play her in the series, would be erected on the Gran Vía. The site was just down the street from the Telefónica building where the Javis had discussed their careers three years before. The poster could be read as a sign both of the new configuration of audiovisual media in Spain, where television and streaming had taken over from the feature film which once dominated the historic picture palaces of the Gran Vía, and of the once marginal Javis' new centrality in the reconfigured entertainment industry.

The distribution of their latest series, which was disrupted by the pandemic, also suggested the fusion or confusion of old and new media. The first two episodes premiered online on Antena 3's premium web player. But they were later shown in socially distanced movie theaters, where they broke attendance records, before finally screening to a general audience on Spanish broadcast TV. In the USA the series would be picked up HBO+, a new upmarket streaming rival to the ubiquitous Netflix, in a sign of the Javis' growing international prestige. Indeed *Veneno* (unlike *Paquita Salas*) was to receive glowing reviews in both the American specialist and generalist press, acclaimed as 'TV's newest global smash' by the *Los Angeles Times* (Zornosa 2020).

Given the challenges posed to the established audiovisual order by the upstart showrunners and their newly ambitious creation, it is no surprise that the reception of the series was mixed in Spain. And I will now take two long-form articles as illustrations of opposing views of *Veneno* and of the Javis' engagement with the social and media history, which the show and its creators present as mutually constituting.

Cristina Ortiz, nicknamed 'La Veneno', was a transgender woman born in 1964 into poverty in rural Andalusia who escaped her repressive village and abusive

FIG. 1.3. Daniela Santiago as the young adult Veneno in the
Javis' drama series of the same name

family for Madrid. There she became a sex worker in the central Parque del Oeste [Western Park], served as a memorable and controversial panelist on late-night TV talk shows in the 1990s, and declined into prison sentences and a mysterious and violent early death in 2016, at the age of just 52. Her life was surely unknown to the fashionable millennials who make up the Javis' target audience. Yet, increasing the viewers' barriers to entry, their series in eight staggered hour-long episodes (interrupted by the pandemic) does not even follow this little-known timeline but rather sketches the halting narrativization of that progression. Jumping backward and forward in time, *Veneno* approaches its historical figure through the struggle of a younger transwoman, Valeria Vegas, to co-write the autobiography of the predecessor with whom she is obsessed. Beyond historical anecdote, then, this is a tale of multiple mediation and of collective self-invention, by several parties (la Veneno, Valeria, and, implicitly, the Javis themselves as queer celebrities).

The positive article by established academic specialist Concepción Cascajosa Virino (2020) is titled '*Veneno*: Quién vive, quién muere, quién cuenta su historia' [*Veneno*: Who Lives, Who Dies, Who Tells Their Story]. Cascajosa begins by making an apparently farfetched connection with Broadway musical *Hamilton*. Both works, she writes, treat lives cut off before their time; both insert historical material into contemporary controversies; and both focus on a legacy that is more reliant on the memories of others (who 'get to tell their story') than on the acts of protagonists who are violently silenced.

Cascajosa places *Veneno* in the context of current trends in television, rather than (as I do) that of the Javis' own previous work. Thus the new project is in a genre recently popular in international markets, the *bioserie*, whose best example would be the self-named series of the Mexican singing star of Spanish descent *Luis Miguel* (Netflix, 2018). Here again there are three parallels between the two works: a disordered chronology; a focus on a problematic mother figure; and a revisiting and resignifying of famous moments of TV history starring their respective subjects. The Javis, however, made two crucial and original decisions. First, they abandoned the total authorial control they had enjoyed with *Paquita Salas*, delegating experienced professionals to write and direct some episodes, as is normal in the case of long-form TV fiction. Second, they did not adapt Valeria Vegas's book itself but turned the series into a 'making of' those memoirs, a lengthy project which stretches from the moment the author as a child glimpses her future heroine on the TV screen to the time her book is finally published, shortly before La Veneno's death.

A further audiovisual mediation is an early Spanish documentary on transwomen, *Vestida de azul* [Dressed in Blue] (Antonio Giménez Rico, 1983). Cascajosa writes that this empathetic feature film opens La Veneno's story up to themes neglected by her somewhat solipsistic memoirs, such as sisterhood and shared domestic space. Moreover *Vestida de azul* also triggers that self-conscious attention to visualizing technologies we saw earlier in *Paquita Salas*. The last episode of *Veneno* begins with Cristina and her friend and housemate Paca la Piraña (who plays herself) discovering a VHS tape of the film. We cut, as in *Paquita Salas* once more, to pastiche credits of the series itself, remade in a '90s style that is reminiscent of the source film.

Obsessive in their attention to media history, the Javis (writes Cascajosa) are nonetheless freed from the heavy inheritance of past Spanish auteur cinema, obsessed as it is with 'religion, sex, and violence'. And their focus on Valeria Vegas, the ultimately successful writer, rather than on La Veneno, the finally tragic performer, offers a possibility of happiness and of second chances for trans people similar to that the Javis previously provided for the shamed actor Anna Allen in *Paquita Salas*. Or again, in the final sequence of the last episode of *Veneno*, which shows the scattering of the protagonist's ashes in the park where she once worked, Valeria reassures a ghostly La Veneno that her often sordid life was in fact 'preciosa' [lovely]. For Cascajosa this comment is a tribute offered by the Javis also to all the forgotten transwomen whose names they have remembered and stories retold, even as their series stresses the unreliability of a narration which passes through multiple mediations.

A further essay written in autumn 2020 contests this rosy view. Elizabeth Duval, a young novelist and cultural critic, traces what she calls the 'trans theology' in the 'gospel' of La Veneno according to Valeria Vegas and the Javis. For Duval, our first vision of the resplendent adult La Veneno, haloed by clients' headlights in the nocturnal park, is a 'Marian apparition'. This is typical of the way that the series' logic is not so much narrative or dramatic as illustrative of a fixed icon or canon (the word 'icon', almost invariably attributed to La Veneno, had originally featured in the working title of the Javis' series).

Duval wonders if it is crueler for the Javis to convert a dead woman into a goddess (as they do) than it was for the TV producers of the '90s to turn a live women into a court jester (as they did). Viewers, Duval suggests, are thus moved not by the story of an individual human but by the depiction of society's mistreatment of a despised collective. La Veneno, she writes, now more Christ than Virgin, 'dies for our sins'. And this theology becomes a teleology: the very television which made her an icon will also, inevitably, destroy her. The problem is, for Duval, that the contemporary fictional series uses manipulative techniques similar to those that it critiques in the exploitative reality television of the past.

Where Cascajosa sees the theme of intergenerational sisterhood as a positive rewriting of a tragic story, then, Duval sees it as an evasion. In spite of what the series tells us, all transwomen are not the same; and Valeria's social embarrassments in a later period (for example, when a relative at a dinner party calls attention to her infertility) are hardly comparable to the mortal dangers faced by La Veneno just twenty years before. For Duval the series thus fails to show how the damage done to La Veneno was not personal or metaphysical (with the star playing the part of the crucified Christ) but rather structural and institutional (martyred by forces intrinsic to television and to the society of the time). The series thus erases history, even as it attempts to repair the damage done by that history; and, offering false consolation, does harm even as it has undeniably done good: by casting trans actors as its trans characters and by making its surviving subjects (like the previously sidelined Paca la Piraña) simply happy.

What is striking, then, in the versions of the series presented by these two critics is that they both locate the supposed success or failure of *Veneno* in its problematic relation to history. For Cascajosa, it retells a valuable and vulnerable story (or history) that is a legacy of collective memory; for Duval, it betrays that story (that history) by abstracting it into a static theology, immune to the troubling vicissitudes of temporal change. Let us now go on, finally, to look at how the text of the series itself addresses this key question.

## *Veneno*: Episode 1

The pre-credit sequence of the opening episode of *Veneno* announces the new cinematic ambitions of the Javis after the low-budget fiction feature *La llamada* and the small-scale, mock documentary *Paquita Salas*. To a dreamy soundtrack of muted trumpet and piano, a child clutching a teddy bear looks through the bannisters. As parents watch a flickering TV set down below, we glimpse (the child glimpses) a red mane of hair and a pair of glossy lips and overhear some enigmatic dialogue ('I always felt like a woman, even when I was a man'). The camera rises above the bannisters, mimicking the child's fascination; and then there is a reverse shot showing the small face, as if caught behind prison bars. The child, still gazing, is swept up by an unseen mother and returned to bed.

This oblique, partial vision of the fascinating figure who gives her name to the series will be repeated throughout the episode. And audiovisual technique will be reinforced by narrative perspectivism. Lengthy titles that follow this sequence make explicit that the series is based on La Veneno's memoirs, co-written with

Valeria Vegas, but also on the accounts of 'those whose lives she changed'. The titles continue by warning that 'memorias' [memories or memoirs] mix reality and fiction; and that, as in all fictional stories, here there is something 'profoundly true'. This is an epistemological skepticism that Cascajosa sees as commemorating a forgotten collective experience and Duval as abstracting that experience into myth.

This opening is set, we are told, in 'Valencia, 1996'. We now cut without explanation to the same city in 2006. Focusing, as in *Paquita Salas*, on visualizing technology, the camera first shows in extreme close-up a decidedly non-smart phone of the period with a primitive video game, 'Snake', on its tiny screen. We pull out to a sordid night scene, its darkness lit by a neon pharmacy sign. The plump, punkish girl shown here is familiar to the audience: she is the favorite actor of the Javis who previously played Paquita's faithless client (Mariona Terés). A shadowy figure now appears, barely lit by a flaming match. It is the now mature La Veneno, obliquely glimpsed for a second time. In a primitive text message of the period, shown in extreme close-up, the girl alerts her best friend Valeria (soon to start her own transition) of her brief encounter with the legendary icon they both adore.

We then cut to the set of a TV talk show where the key figure will be a journalist, Faela, played by Almodóvar regular Lola Dueñas, a sign of the Javis' new ability to cast major actors in principal roles. Recently returned from maternity leave, Faela is dismayed to find her place taken by a younger, cuter colleague 'so dumb she slept with the writer'. Television, then, is a merciless arena in which professionals, as much as performers, are subject to ruthless competition and exploitation; and in which women are patronized and diminished by their male counterparts. As the episode develops, the narrative focus will oscillate between Faela, a desperate TV journalist in 1996, and Valeria, a troubled student journalist in 2006, and their clashing views of the compelling, vulnerable figure that both are hunting down in different decades.

The discourse on media effects is very explicit in this opening episode. Valeria attends a lecture where her journalism professor speaks on the role of media in enforcing social control and excluding marginal subjects. (At the end of the episode Valeria's paper for this course will be acclaimed as a first draft of her book.) In troubling evidence of the consequences of media-enabled celebrity, we are shown characters watching on television the distraught fans of British boy band Take That and of Spanish singer Rocío Jurado, who was at that time on her death bed (both are referenced in *Paquita Salas*). Flash-lit fame is thus not always to be preferred to the anonymity of the shadows. And a lengthy, disturbing sequence that is central to the episode (halfway through its running time, essential to its main thesis on media) explores this paradox of visibility and invisibility.

Having literally crashed into a group of rowdy transgender sex workers, Faela, desperate to get on air, takes her cameraman to their sordid park (which actually features a picturesque rose garden and Egyptian temple unseen in the episode). It is here that La Veneno makes a third appearance, resplendent in a revealing scarlet gown, and this time as the Marian apparition critiqued by Duval. Yet we know from *La llamada* that the Javis take Catholic iconography seriously. And unlike the modestly silent Virgin, La Veneno has a ready wit, responding in kind to Faela's salacious questions (on the definition and cost of 'French' and 'Greek') and claiming to have a 'shark' in her underwear.

But soon things get dangerous. Faela is surrounded by a menacing circle of sex workers who summon their armed pimp, demanding the videotape that she and the cameraman have just shot and whose footage we have seen through the viewfinder in its vintage Academy ratio (once more, that attention to technology). The women insist that, working at the job that they do, they cannot afford to be shown on screen and recognized by their families. And they threaten to kill Faela. It is a tour de force dramatic scene, without a flicker of humor, such as the Javis have never attempted before.

The episode then crosscuts between the Faela and Valeria plotlines, suggesting disturbing parallels between them. After all, the first is complicit in the exploitations of reality TV, newly crude in the '90s, while the second is devout in her worship of an icon whose memoirs she will much later faithfully offer to the world. Yet both women are shown wearily returning at night to their modest homes, blurring the decade-long time difference between them. The unusual crosscutting here is anachronistic as, according to the logic of continuity editing, it would normally serve to signal simultaneity.

In spite of this critique of the deadly effects of mass media *Veneno*, like *Paquita Salas* and *La llamada*, will stress finally female solidarity: Faela will band together with her younger rival to procure the voluble La Veneno as a valuable (profitable) guest on her show; Valeria will gain entrance to the warm domestic space which La Veneno shares with her eternal friend Paca la Piraña. And in this latter sequence we are finally shown La Veneno in the merciless light of day. Hearing that now rare fans have called for her, she stumbles outside, overweight and middle-aged, still clad in her pajamas. There could hardly be a more different and pathetic sight to that of the regal figure we have previously glimpsed in the nocturnal park and on late-night television.

La Veneno now reviews a cherished photo album with Valeria, visual testimony to a lost life (a life lost?) in the media spotlight. And she is the first person to recognize the pre-transitioning Valeria who has not yet picked out that female name as trans, asking 'What about you?' But this rhetoric of interiority ('It's something you've always carried inside') is belied by the spectacular and ever-changing body of Cristina/La Veneno in the photos. This body could be described in the same words the Javis, in a final disclaimer, use of their series: it is the 'result of creative development'.

Still the first episode, surprisingly focalized on and through two relatively minor figures (the TV journalist and the student memoirist), insists on the plurality and obliqueness of its and their vision. There are thus two climaxes at the end. As mentioned earlier, Valeria's professor sees her term paper on La Veneno as the germ of a book, a recognition that is as much a revelation to its future author as is her trans identity; but simultaneously (ten years earlier) Faela sees her discovery La Veneno make a first, clamorous and dangerous, appearance on set, an appearance which vindicates Faela's own professional skill. In both cases the camera focuses on the faces of the creators, entranced by their own media work, and not on the inspiration of that work: La Veneno who remains, still, even after a full hour of drama as elusive and as potent as the 'shark' she says she bears between her legs.

## History, Genealogy, Theology

The second episode of *Veneno* takes viewers on an extended return to its subject's brutal and memorable childhood in Andalusia. But both opening episodes remained isolated from the rest by the production delay imposed by the pandemic. After their successful premiere on Antena 3's premium platform, these first episodes were accorded special status, screened in movie theaters and broadcast on national television. This fragmented and multiple vision (of its distribution, of its text) continues until the end of the series. The eighth and last episode, featuring all three actors who play the adult La Veneno, is called 'Los tres entierros de Cristina Ortiz' [The Three Burials of Cristina Ortiz].

The fact that in real life La Veneno has been granted a commemorative plaque in the park where she once worked suggests that her life story has indeed been rescued by those who have retold it and by those who, as the Javis wrote in their credits, have been affected by it. And in spite of its new-scale, professional production values, and international reach, *Veneno* has much in common with *La llamada* and *Paquita Salas*, not least in its evident affection for its troubled subject. Moreover the Javis' sympathetic treatment of actors was tested as never before by members of the *Veneno* cast whose own real-life transition process did not always coincide with that of their fictional characters.

As *Cinemanía*'s unsympathetic critic wrote with unexpected insight of their feature film, in spite of an apparent campiness the Javis scorn the luxury of cheap irony; and, as Cascajosa commented, they are untroubled by the historical burden of Spanish auteur cinema with its still traumatizing burden of religion, sex, and violence. It is perhaps for this reason that, when they could have surely done otherwise, given the backing of American giants Netflix and HBO, the Javis chose to continue to work primarily on and for Spanish television and its associated local streaming platforms. And although they had already made a successful feature film they did not flee to the more prestigious heritage medium of cinema. After all, TV is the cherished domestic resource which they (like Paquita and Valeria) learned to love as vulnerable children.

The Javis are clearly as media savvy as their heroines, carefully nurturing their own press coverage. When I met the charming couple after their event at the Telefónica they told me they were familiar with an English-language article I had recently published on their work. Yet even they have had their challenges on social media, with one of the couple withdrawing from Twitter, hurt by haters. We should not then minimize the Javis' achievement by claiming that, unlike in previous decades, queer content such as theirs is now safe, no longer transgressive.

If that is indeed the case in Spain, then it is partly because of their own brave visibility as a media couple in the brightest and most unforgiving of spotlights. And by lovingly exploring the image repertoire of the past, Javier Calvo and Javier Ambrossi have forged a genealogy of LGBTQ expression that is 'theological' only in the sense that it displays a devout reverence for those once fragile and ephemeral icons who have inspired them. It is a reverence recreated from the perspective of a present that is ever renewed.

## References: Text

CASCAJOSA VIRINO, CONCEPCIÓN. 2020. '*Veneno*: Quién vive, quién muere, quién cuenta su historia', *Serializados*, October <https://serielizados.com/veneno-quien-vive-quien-muere-quien-cuenta-tu-historia/> [accessed 10 February 2021]

DUVAL, ELIZABETH. 2020. 'Teología "trans": el evangelio de La Veneno según Valeria Vegas (y los Javis)', *CTXT: Contexto y Acción*, 21 November <https://ctxt.es/es/20201101/Culturas/34171/veneno-serie-evangelio-valeria-vegas-elizabeth-duval.htm> [accessed 10 February 2021]

GARCÍA, YAGO. 2017. REVIEW OF *La llamada*, *Cinemanía*, 7 August <http://cinemania.elmundo.es/peliculas/la-llamada/critica/> [accessed 10 February 2021]

MORATE, MAITE. 2017. 'Los Javis, una imparable revolución "millennial"', *El País*, 24 December

REDACCIÓN BARCELONA. 2017. 'Echanove habla sobre su despido de *Cuéntame*: "No me han dicho ni adiós"', *La Vanguardia*, 27 March <https://www.lavanguardia.com/series/20170327/421232489033/juan-echanove-despedido-cuentame.html>

SÁNCHEZ CASTREJÓN, PEDRO. 2017. *Todo sobre mi Madrid* (Madrid: La Librería)

VALTUEÑA, DANIEL. 2020. 'Lorca, Almodóvar, y los Javis: dispositivo y genealogía de la creación homosexual en España', unpublished article.

ZORNOSA, LAURA. 2020. 'How the Trans Icon that Spaniards "Didn't Want to See" Inspired TV's Newest Global Smash', *Los Angeles Times*, 19 November <https://www.latimes.com/entertainment-arts/tv/story/2020–11–19/la-veneno-hbo-max-cristina-ortiz-transgender-icon> [accessed 10 February 2021]

## References: Audiovisual

*Belle époque*. 1992. Dir. by Fernando Trueba (Animatógrafo)

*Blancanieves*. 2012. Dir. by Pablo Berger (Arcadia Motion Pictures)

*Chicas de hoy en día*. 1991–92. (El Catalejo/RTVE)

*chicas del cable, Las*. 2017–20. (Bambú/Netflix)

*Cuéntame cómo pasó*. 2001–present. (Grupo Ganga/RTVE)

*Entre tinieblas*. 1983. Dir. by Pedro Almodóvar (Tesauro)

*Física o química*. 2008–11. (Ida y Vuelta/Antena 3)

*Hable con ella*. 2002. Dir. by Pedro Almodóvar (El Deseo)

*Ley del deseo*. 1987. Dir. by Pedro Almodóvar (El Deseo)

*llamada, La*. 2017. Dir. by Javier Ambrossi and Javier Calvo (Apache Films)

*Luis Miguel*. 2018. (Gato Grande/Canana/Netflix)

*Médico de familia*. 1995–99. (Globomedia/Telecinco)

*olivo, El*. 2016. Dir. by Icíar Bollaín (Morena Films)

*Operación Triunfo*. 2001. (Gestmusic/TVE)

*Paquita Salas*. 2016–present. (Flooxer/Neox/Netflix)

*secreto de Puente Viejo, El*. 2011–present. (Boomerang/Ida Y Vuelta/Antena 3)

*Todo sobre mi madre.* 1999. Dir. by Pedro Almodóvar (El Deseo)
*Veneno.* 2020. (Atresmedia Studios/HBO Max)
*Vestida de azul.* 1983. Dir. by Antonio Giménez Rico (Serva Films)
*Volver.* 2006. Dir. by Pedro Almodóvar (El Deseo)

# CHAPTER 2

# Twenty-first-century Lorca: Historical Memory and Heritage in Theater, Cinema, and Television

## Lorca's Legacies

Historical memory has of course been a central topic for Peninsular studies in general and more particularly for the *Journal of Spanish Cultural Studies*, which has tasked itself over some twenty years with remaking the discipline. While Jo Labanyi's article of 2008 ('The Politics of Memory in Contemporary Spain') remains influential, José Colmeiro's review of 2018 ('Unraveling Memories in Spain') covers no fewer than four books on the topic.

While historical memory, so amply treated elsewhere, is not a main theme of my book, this second chapter treats three texts in different media whose creators do to some extent invoke that subject. Their main aim is to refashion for the new context of the twenty-first century a key figure already mentioned in the first chapter: Federico García Lorca. Coincidentally, all three were premiered in 2015, that is four years before the Javis' reimagining of rural tragedy *La casa de Bernarda Alba* [The House of Bernarda Alba] via urban comedy *Paquita Salas*. And they share with the Javis a willingness to propose a radical revision of Lorca's legacy or, more properly, legacies.

Alberto Conejero's play *La piedra oscura* [The Dark Stone] stages an imaginary conversation between Lorca's last lover, Rafael Rodríguez Rapún, and the guard in the prison where he is interned before execution by the Nationalists. Based, according to the author's own account, on research on the particular sources for the play and more generally on the concept of historical memory, the play stresses the queer component of Lorca's heritage, even as the poet himself is conspicuously absent from the stage.

Paula Ortiz's feature film *La novia* [The Bride] is a rewriting of Lorca's play *Bodas de sangre* [Blood Wedding] from the perspective of the main female character. Reworking Lorca's alleged affinity with women, central to his historical memory, the film offers an explicitly feminist account of a problematic patriarchal society, avoiding folklore by translating the play to an abstract landscape (the film was partly shot in Turkey) and an unspecified period (the film features both elemental horses and time-bound twentieth-century motorbikes).

Finally, *El Ministerio del Tiempo* [The Ministry of Time] is a prize-winning science fiction TV series which aired on national public channel TVE. As a climax to its first season, the last episode is devoted to the young Lorca, lodging famously in the Residencia de Estudiantes [Student Hall of Residence] with Buñuel and Dalí. Here most explicitly the historical memory of cultural heritage is juxtaposed with the lived reality of modern Spain: the contemporary characters engage with a character from the past who prefigures the progressive changes of the present, yet will not himself benefit from them.

While all three texts raise similar questions as to the dialogue between past and present, history and contemporaneity, I will argue that it is the last that, through the domestic distribution of television also of course favored by the Javis, most deftly incorporates memory into the fabric of everyday life for modern Spanish audiences.

First, however, I would like briefly to address what María Delgado has called the 'after lives' of Lorca (2008: 173–201) in the post-Franco period immediately before my own. While the bibliography on the poet-dramatist is immense, there is much less on the fictional depiction of his historical figure, which is what concerns me here. And perhaps the most interesting survey of that field is by Alberto Mira, the most prolific and expert scholar on LGBTQ cultural history in Spain. Moreover Mira's main point is one that anticipates my own later texts: it is the conspicuous absence of the twentieth century's most celebrated Spanish author in texts from the '70s, '80s, and '90s that claim to commemorate him. Rarely and valuably, also, Mira deals with television as well as film.

Mira's first work (which he takes out of chronological order) is veteran anti-Francoist filmmaker Juan Antonio Bardem's *Lorca, muerte de un poeta* [Lorca, Death of a Poet] (1987), a co-production with Italy's public TV service RAI. This was made as a television miniseries of six hour-long episodes, but cut down to two hours for a theatrical feature release focused on its subject's death, as cited in its title. Mira sketches the televisual context. This miniseries was one of state Televisión Española's self-dubbed 'classics' (a genre I treat in Chapter 4 of this book) whose prestige is signaled by the cultural cachet of its production team: the respected director, established members of the cast, and the team of screenwriters (who included scholarly biographer Ian Gibson) (2007: 124).

Rejecting as it does the model of the Hollywood biopic, in which historical details are subordinated to an inflexible narrative arc, the series is structured around a void: Lorca, writes Mira, 'remains the passive centre of events; he moves from one famous location to another and things just happen to him' (2007: 124). (We might add that there is also an intrusive Voice of God narration, which seeks to establish places and faces which are not clear within the diegesis itself.) And if narrative causality is lost, then so is that other staple of Hollywood storytelling, psychological motivation.

It comes as a surprise when, in a late episode, Lorca is heard making an anguished confession of homosexuality to a friend, a theme that had gone unmentioned before, even in the episode devoted to his famously close association with Dalí (2007: 125). This confessional moment is taken from Gibson's biography, where it is presented, however, as being from a somewhat unreliable source. Yet Mira does not question the scene's potential lack of historical accuracy in presenting the confession as true, but rather its lack of consistency within the story world: 'the choice they must make', he writes of the series' creators, 'is not between truth and drama, but between consistent narrative, true to character, and the inconsistent collection of moments in the life of a writer' (2007: 125).

It is of course no accident that this trouble in representation should arise here around the debated question of homosexuality, which remains something of an embarrassment to the Marxist Bardem. And Mira's next two texts exhibit similar troubling discontinuities and inconsistencies.

First, Marcos Zurinaga's aptly named *The Disappearance of García Lorca* (1997) (also known as *Death in Granada*) is at once a feature film in the genre of the thriller and a 'quest for [the] truth' of Lorca's death (2007: 126), a death which is, as in Bardem's series, taken problematically to be the key to and culmination of Lorca's life. Exiled in Puerto Rico as a child after the Civil War, the protagonist Ricardo returns to Granada in 1958. His aim is to make investigations into a situation likely to be long familiar to Spanish audiences on the release of the film, not least through the extensive writings of Gibson, who is once more given a script credit here.

Again the question of sexuality is troubling: while in the film (the fictional) Ricardo barely met the (real-life) poet (although he remains haunted by his memory), his father shared an ambiguous special friendship with Lorca when both were teenagers in Granada. Through such dramatic devices *The Disappearance of García Lorca* thus achieves some of the tension absent in the reverent waxworks of *Lorca, muerte de un poeta*. But it does so only at the cost of displacing history into metaphorical abstraction and distracting anachronism: the quest for Lorca 'becomes an illustration of the impossibility to recover the past'; and the conspicuous casting of Cuban exile Andy Garcia as Lorca (Bardem's protagonist had been played yet more incongruously by an Englishman) blurs the differences between anti-Francoism and anti-Castroism (2007: 127).

Finally, and more satisfactorily, Mira examines a chronologically early text, Jaime Chávarri's enigmatic art movie *A un dios desconocido* [To An Unknown God] (1977). In this psychological drama an older man returns once more to the Granada where forty years before he had been in love with another youth. Here the presence of Lorca is yet more attenuated: he registers only as a visitor playing the piano as heard by the boys from a garden on an idyllic summer afternoon in 1936 (2007: 127). Although much more complex, *A un dios desconocido* shares strategies with the simpler thriller *The Disappearance of García Lorca*: the writer is represented only through 'the impact he has on someone else's life'; and Lorca's influence is shown only as 'an inheritance from the pre-Civil War years' (2007: 127). Daringly, however, here a gay sex act (fellatio), albeit not carried out by Lorca himself, is presented as the 'transmission of tradition and knowledge' from past to present (2007: 127).

Mira concludes that Lorca himself 'is treated as icon; his legacy makes sense only in terms of the way other characters conceive of it' (2007: 128). This is a curious anticipation of another queer bio-series, the *Veneno* we examined in the last chapter.

And it is a strategy of displacement that we will also find in my more recent texts, which are, unsurprisingly perhaps with the passing of time, more daring and creative in their employment of revision and anachronism.

## Three Lorcas Three

Since its first production on 14 January 2015 at Madrid's public theater which forms part of the Centro Dramático Nacional [National Dramatic Center] and is named for nineteenth-century actor-producer María Guerrero, Alberto Conejero's two-handed play *La piedra oscura* has been frequently produced around the Spanish-speaking world from Mexico City to Lima. At the time of writing the expert Mexican version from the 2019 season is available at full length on YouTube (KO-Z Producciones 2020). I myself heard Conejero's text in a staged reading in New York's Instituto Cervantes in 2018.

While its author has stressed in the foreword to the play his immersion in textual and oral sources of historical memory, including original interviews with Rodríguez Rapún's surviving family (Conejero 2016: 17–18), the premise of his work is avowedly ahistorical, resting as it does on the fictitious suggestion that Rapún survived the air raid that killed him in Santander and was rather imprisoned and executed days later by the victorious Francoists. Conejero also invents Rapún's interlocutor in the play, the teenage guard whose name is belatedly revealed as 'Sebastián'.

Critics have made explicit the play's connection with and contribution to the historical memory debate. Surprisingly perhaps, the script of this counterfactual drama was published with a laudatory preface by Ian Gibson, who is, as mentioned earlier, the historian best known for his attempt to ascertain the irrefutable facts of Lorca's disputed death and burial place over the course of some forty years. Gibson writes at one point, intervening in current party politics:

> A su manera la empresa de Conejero encaja dentro del movimiento por la recuperación de la memoria histórica, movimiento tan necesario para la salud del país y calificado calumniosamente por la derecha como intento de 'reabrir heridas', cuando estas nunca se han cerrado. (Conejero 2016: 13)

> [In its own way Conejero's project fits into the movement for the recovery of historical memory, a movement which is so necessary for the health of the country and has been slanderously described the Right as an attempt to 'reopen wounds', although those wounds have never healed.]

Press reception also called attention to those same wounds, but citing the specificity of the theater medium. A report ahead of the premiere in *El País*, titled 'Encuentro con el enemigo' [Encounter with the Enemy], quotes Conejero on what he prefers to call 'collective' (rather than 'historical') memory (García 2015). The dramaturge claims further that his play promotes 'redemption' through the Other and the capacity of language to be 'sanadora' [healing], even 'salvadora' [life-saving]. Likewise, the Argentine director of the play, Pablo Messiez, suggests that *La piedra oscura* transcends the past:

FIG. 2.1. A scene from the first production of *La piedra oscura* at
Madrid's María Guerrero theater

> Más allá de un trabajo arqueológico y de investigación sobre la historia, lo
> importante es dejarse llevar por la situación presente entre estas dos personas
> que viven ante el espectador esa necesidad de encuentro profundo y verdadero
> entre ellas. (García 2015)

> [Over and above a work of archeology and historical research, the important
> thing is to let yourself be carried away by the present situation of the these two
> people, who experience in front of the audience the need for a deep and true
> encounter with one another.]

This 'encounter' is exemplified by the characters' final embrace, after which the
two ex-enemies are now 'difficult to separate'.

It is a physicality recreated more bloodily by the conditions of spectatorship
contrived for the performance: Messiez hung shirts, described in the article
as blood- and wound-stained, over the backs of each of the seats in the small
auditorium, arguing that 'para ver esta función hay que sentarse sobre una ausencia'
[to see this performance you have to be sitting on an absence]. It is an absence
repeated, of course, in the refusal to depict Lorca himself on stage, one we saw
earlier in cinematic approximations to the poet such as *A un dios desconocido*. Messiez
further suggests that this play embodies the essence of theater, namely 'repetir cada
noche las palabras para que la historia no se olvide' [repeat the words every night so
that history (or perhaps 'the story') is not forgotten]. The successive performances of
the play thus serve in themselves as a kind of insistent memory mechanism.

*La piedra oscura*'s minimalist *mise en scène* (two actors, one set, no intermission) no
doubt also facilitated the many productions around the world that followed the first

in the María Guerrero, as well as reinforcing the play's stark theatricality. The work lost little of its dramatic effect in the staged reading I saw in New York. And, also in 2018, Lima's small Teatro Lucía even recycled the play's set in their next production, which was coincidentally another two-handed imaginary homoerotic encounter, this time between Sor Juana Inés de la Cruz and Frida Kahlo.

But *La piedra oscura*'s success rests mainly on its recreation of the seduction that the historical Lorca exercised over his contemporaries (and, indeed, modern Spaniards) by transposing that attraction onto the fragile relationship it creates between Rapún and Sebastián. The first man thus comes slowly to confess his love for the poet and the second to accede to Rapún's request that he retrieve Lorca's private papers from their safe place in Madrid. This threatened archive would include both lost letters between the lovers and the real-life lost Lorca play (also known as *La bola negra* [The Black Ball]) from which Conejero derives the title of his own work.

If historicity is blurred, transmuted into the temporally and spatially abstracted space of the stage, homosexuality is also transposed into a broader and more fragile mode of homoeroticism: the couple, neither of whom identifies as gay, barely touch throughout the play (as mentioned before, they do embrace in the final scene) and engage most deeply with each other only on a verbal level (the play has almost no physical action).

This theme of the archive as fragile connection between past and present recurs in the playwright's incorporation of texts by Lorca himself into his own, most especially with one of the *Sonetos del amor oscuro* [Sonnets of Dark Love] that is recited in its entirety. Suggesting that the conflictive and conflicted figure of Lorca need no longer be directly represented (although his words are spoken intermittently in the play by a disembodied 'Voz' [Voice]), Conejero thus displaces the memory of the poet's creativity and homosexuality onto the twin protagonists of his drama, implicitly projecting that trace into a queer future. This sense or promise of futurity is clearest in Rapún's last speech, which looks forward to the twenty-first-century movement to disinter collective graves, citing the 'thousands of eyes' which will observe those who shed the blood of Lorca when the poet's body is discovered and properly reburied.

Let us look more closely at the scene of the sonnet. In the sixth of the play's eight short scenes, Rapún refuses to see a priest before his execution but instead makes a lengthy confession to the young soldier (Conejero 2016: 82–84). Rapún's 'sin' is that he let Lorca return to Granada rather than insisting he stay with him. Rapún also recounts to Sebastián both the intoxicating fascination with Lorca that led him to surrender sexually to him and his fear of homophobic gossip when he found himself identified as the poet's 'boy' or 'companion' and heard bystanders utter the word 'maricón' [queer].

It is in this context that Rapún begins to recite the sonnet titled 'El amor duerme en el pecho del poeta' [Love Sleeps on the Breast of the Poet] (84–85). Its first lines 'Tú nunca entenderás lo que te quiero | porque duermes en mí y estás dormido' [You will never understand how I love you | because you are sleeping in me and you are asleep] are now redirected by Rapún, formerly the unconscious recipient

FIG. 2.2. Álex García as Leonardo and Inma Cuesta as the
Bride in Paula Ortiz's feature film *La novia*

of Lorca's verse, to Sebastián, the equally unknowing receiver of this amorous discourse. Both the mobility of subject and object (a poem from the poet to his love object repurposed as a confession from that love object to his captor) and the dexterity with which the authentic text of the poem is woven into the imagined dialogue of the play are striking here. They suggest a fluid fusion that dissolves boundaries of time, space, and person and a re-appropriation of the historical figure of Lorca, which is also seen in the other works I treat in this chapter.

My second text, *La novia*, is, as mentioned earlier, a film adaptation of Lorca's 1932 play *Bodas de sangre*. The change in the title here signals a new female focus from a woman director. Paula Ortiz also cast a TV star, Inma Cuesta, to promote public recognition: although Cuesta has taken roles in films, she was more widely known to afternoon audiences for Spanish period serials such as *Amar en tiempos revueltos* [Loving in Troubled Times] (TVE, 2005–12), where she played the central role in her season as an initially shy girl who finally succeeds in her ambition of becoming a cabaret singer, in spite of her family's disapproval. This serial was set in the Civil War and early Francoist era (Luisa Gavasa, the Mother in *La novia*, played the matriarch in the same show). Cuesta was thus already endowed with an intimate connection to the female televisual audience and with the genre of costume drama. Although romantically hirsute Álex García as Leonardo has roughly the same degree of celebrity as his co-star, the Spanish poster features only a close up of an anguished Cuesta looking straight into the camera.

Unfaithful to its original, *La novia*'s production design rejects the style of Andalusian folklore with which Lorca is so often tricked out, on screen as on stage. It favors rather a more florid version of the somewhat austere abstraction we saw earlier in *La piedra oscura*. The rural tragedy of adultery and assassination is thus shot here in stylized settings: the climactic wedding takes place in an abandoned building that stands in a blasted landscape and the bride later flees with her lover on horseback through the phallic rock formations of Cappadocia, Turkey, far from

Lorca's Andalusia. *La novia* thus retools the literary adaptation, long a staple of Spanish cinema that has latterly fallen out of fashion, just as it offers a new reading of a classic text.

Critics in Spain and elsewhere did not, however, respond positively to Ortiz's innovations, which were held to be a betrayal of the original text. On the film's limited theatrical release *El País*, once more, spoke of 'Lorca de diseño' [Lorca by design] arguing that 'Paula Ortiz ha preferido intentar atrapar lo bello. Y lo malo de aspirar a lo bello es que te puedes quedar en su simulacro' [Paula Ortiz has preferred to try to trap the beautiful. And the drawback of aiming for the beautiful is that you can end up with a fake] (Ocaña 2015).

For the reviewer, then, the film is false because it is overly decorative. And this judgment (at once artistic, moral, and political) is based on the adaptation's supposed deviation from the received figure of Lorca that the critic takes upon himself to define: 'Lorca es popular, recio, amargo. Esta película es remilgada, bonita en el sentido más subjetivo de la palabra, presuntamente estilosa...' [Lorca belongs to the people, he is harsh, bitter. This film is affected, pretty in the most subjective sense of the word, pretentiously stylish]. The journalist cites here the scene of the knife fight that he claims is fought with daggers that look like they come from Lladró, the Valencian manufacturer of kitsch figurines. While clearly this critique is gendered (contrasting as it does masculine austerity with feminine frivolity), it also invokes the author function in classic Foucaldian style in order to police the interpretation of a canonical text. Foreign critics echoed the charge. Reviewing the film on its world premiere at the San Sebastián International Film Festival, *Variety* wrote that *La novia* was 'decorative but inessential', comparing its style to that of the (female-targeted) genres of soap opera and telenovela (Lodge 2015). *Variety* also laments the anachronistic elements in the production design and soundtrack which mean the film 'does not speak to any clear cultural moment'. The contrast with the stripped-down, male-dominated and historically contextualized *La piedra oscura*, which was much better received, is evident.

It is true that *La novia* replays in an aestheticized and abstract mode tropes lodged in Spanish and international audiences' memories as key to Lorca and often vulnerable to stereotypical gender interpretation. Thus, we are given many handsome shots of raging (male) stallions and ominous (female) moons. Yet, although there are some scenes of female nudity (Cuesta is shown topless), it is the male body that is most exposed to the spectator's gaze. And the climactic knife fight between the two rival lovers, which is of course unseen in the play itself, is here shot with clear homoerotic intent, especially as a smoldering Álex García is asked to play the scene clad only in a shirt. The male body thus substitutes for the female as primary object of desire for the protagonist as for the target audience.

This scene, which was singled out for ridicule by *El País*'s reviewer, is more complex formally than it first appears. It is preceded by a lengthy sequence of lovemaking in the forest where Leonardo is nude but the Bride is provided with lacy lingerie. Dialogue here is shot discontinuously with the soundtrack, at some times synchronous with the actors' lip movements but at others not. Moreover, the love scene is interrupted by disorientating cutaways which show the Old Woman (who is not present at the action) mouthing the lines of both characters. When the Bridegroom arrives on his sputtering motorbike (the lovers had come by a more elemental horse), Leonardo pauses to barely button his shirt before engaging his rival in battle, naked from the waist down. The duration of this sequence plays out to a somewhat incongruous song (to which I refer below), further distancing viewers from the assumed period of the action. The fight is crosscut with close ups of the Bride and Old Woman which read as point of view shots for the unfolding homoerotic action. Finally, the Bride interposes herself between the two men's bodies, now lethally embraced.

*Variety* wrote sympathetically of this sequence that 'The most gracious nod to Lorca's legacy may be the anachronistic inclusion of the Leonard Cohen song "Take This Waltz", the lyrics of which were adapted from [...] *Poet in New York*' (Lodge 2015). While, unlike the print shown at San Sebastián, the final cut of the film featured not Cohen's original but a Spanish version of his adaptation of the poem, Ortiz's use of this song suggests, like her *mise en scène*, a fluid displacement of Lorca's text in time, place, and even language. We might compare the song's incorporation into *La novia* to that of the sonnet in *La piedra oscura* in the scene studied earlier.

Ortiz's staging of the men's knife fight thus establishes through its shooting style the female spectator as voyeur. And her most significant change to the play's plot sets up a kind of women's time which transcends the chronological sequence of male history and its linear mode of memory. Thus, the old gypsy woman who represents Death and appears three times in the play's final act is at the end of the film identified with the *novia* herself, reduced as she is to a barely recognizable abject state. The film's enigmatic opening sequence, which is absent in Lorca's play, shows the Bride with her wedding gown ragged and mud-caked about to turn into the Old Woman. It is an identification confirmed in the last shot of the film where the young woman morphs into her senior version. In this revision, then, the female figure is no longer the passive bystander of a tragic episode (the elopement and double murder) but rather an active presence that precedes and succeeds that discrete event, establishing a kind of temporal continuum before and after the familiar narrative. It is a feminist statement that versions of Lorca in previous decades did not think to make.

That continuum is also suggested by television series *El Ministerio del Tiempo*, the most prestigious and original series produced for TVE in some years, not least in its pioneering engagement with digital media beyond the broadcast medium. Spanish scholar Ana María Castillo Hinojosa has discerned four characteristics of television drama as 'object of exchange' on the Internet: the creative expression of identity, the search for empathy, group membership, and, our main interest here, collective memory (2012: 911). This is clearly the case with *El Ministerio del Tiempo* which, beyond its meticulously crafted primary text, knowingly extended its brand in order to create a viewing community. The sheer number of creative works inspired by the series is overwhelming, as can be seen by the analysis of this phenomenon in the book edited by Concepción Cascajosa Virino (2015), the same scholar who would place the Javis' *Veneno* in the context of the history of Spanish television. Such elaborate fan fictions and pictures attest to the creation of a new community of collective memory, attached both to the series itself and to the contested national history on which it draws. Indeed, blurring the boundary between production and consumption, some of those most active in the fan community were taken on in later seasons of the show as members of its multimedia creative team.

With reference to memory, we find here, as might be expected in a time-travel narrative, a temporal confusion or collision in the series' text, in this case the presence of the past in the present. This conflict is embodied by the three protagonists from the first season, who are temporally and geographically diverse: twentieth-century Madrid nurse Julián, nineteenth-century Barcelona student Amelia, and sixteenth-century soldier Alonso, who is first seen in Flanders. But temporal conflict is also embedded in the main premise of the series, the struggle to preserve a shared national history that must not be subject to change. This is the mission of the eponymous secret Spanish government agency.

Appropriate for the times of crisis in which it was created and broadcast, *El Ministerio del Tiempo* does not permit itself the reassuring pleasures of nationalism. There are frequent and ironical references to the supposed faults of Spaniards, such as bumbling improvisation. Cascajosa Virino even employs this phrase from the series' dialogue ('Somos españoles: improvisen') [We're Spaniards: improvise] as the title for the introduction to her volume (2015: ix). Episodes typically focus not on national successes but on inglorious or shameful moments of Spanish history: the Inquisition and the picaresque hero, the wreck of the Invincible Armada in the sixteenth century, and the undistinguished reign of Isabel II in the nineteenth. It is characteristic that the young Lope de Vega, a literary figure as canonical as Lorca, is depicted in one episode as an inveterate womanizer, even as the female-led team attempt to save the future national treasure from premature death.

The first season of the series gives off a strong sense of melancholy. This culminates in the final episode, the object of my attention here, which, as mentioned earlier, is set in the Residencia de Estudiantes, a charged and picturesque place of memory that featured heavily as a location in the bio-series of an earlier decade, *Lorca, muerte de un poeta*. The regular cast, who have come from the future, here become intimate with Lorca, who appears only in this climactic episode, but are not allowed to warn him of a murder already anticipated by the poet himself. The confrontation between past and present is initiated by the anachronistic inclusion of an iPad in a Dalí painting from the 1920s. It will involve a clash between the progressive values of present Spain, at least as portrayed in the series, and the memories of past prejudices, most specifically of homophobia, that are shown to be no longer acceptable today.

The relationship between the modern character Julián and the series' version of Lorca is thus based not only on the former's awareness of the latter's mortality (a kind of future in the past) but also on the latter's supposed intuition of social change to come long after his death. It is characteristic of his unique status (in Spanish cultural history, in the series) that Lorca is the one historical character in *El*

*Ministerio del Tiempo* to recognize that the Ministry's functionaries have come from the future and to understand what that means for himself and his country.

No fewer than three scholarly essays in Cascajosa Virino's volume on the series focus on the theme of memory, the last of which treats the final Lorca episode. Óscar González Camaño begins by citing the Ministry's mission: 'evitar que alguien reescriba nuestro pasado y preservar nuestra memoria histórica' [to stop anyone rewriting our past and to preserve our historical memory] (2015: 59). The series thus constructs a 'place of memory' that refers to a 'collective imaginary' (2015: 59). Yet in spite of a succession of constitutional laws, writes González Camaño, there is no 'uniform education' in Spain (2015: 60); and the series' characters reveal varying degrees of knowledge and ignorance of the nation's cultural heritage (2015: 61). Moreover, each has a contradictory view of Spanish history, alternately utopian, revisionist, or fatalistic: the soldier dreams of martial heroism, the student stresses an incipient liberalism fueled by education, and the paramedic is reconciled to a more ambivalent democratic present (2015: 63). González Camaño ends his study of the series by citing novelist Arturo Pérez Reverte on the supposed 'uselessness' of the Law of Historical Memory, but also historian Justo Serna on the 'modest' and 'ironic' viewpoint required of modern Spaniards when they look at their ancestors (2015: 64). The series' 'look from history', then, avoids facile nostalgia.

In a second essay Víctor Mora Gaspar treats history and memory as 'traces and signs' that serve to construct national identity (2015: 77). The great discovery of the series is thus the 'coexistence of multiple temporalities' (2015: 77) which generate (against the Ministry's avowed mission) a 'permanent possibility for change'. Here too nostalgia is not to be dismissed but serves rather as a mechanism for 'building a narratable identity', for characters as for viewers (2015: 79). And while 'institutional memory' does indeed tend to produce 'silences', the latter can be 'filled' or 'resignified' (2015: 82), caught as they are unstably between traces of the past and signs of the future. The moral of the series, then, is that a knowledge of the historical past should be 'in constant revision' and 'open to change' (2015: 83).

While the first two essays cite Lope de Vega as an example of institutional or canonical memory (even as his reputation is humorously undermined by the series), the third focuses on Lorca. Yolanda Cruz offers a close reading of the Residencia de Estudiantes episode focusing on 'theater, cinema, and poetry in the service of the Ministry' (2015: 115). Citing the poem that opens the third act of *Así que pasen cinco años* [When Five Years Have Passed], the episode is called 'La leyenda del tiempo' [The Legend of Time]. The word 'sueño' [sleep or dream] is central to the poem and Cruz notes how, unlike other characters in the series, safely confined to their historical moment, Lorca travels freely into the present via dreams. Thus, as Julián sits on a bench in modern Madrid, the camera pans slightly to the left and Lorca appears in the frame in period dress, 'irrupting' into what will prove to be Julián's dream (2015: 117).

Later, as Cruz notes, it is Julián who appears in Lorca's dream, thus enabling the poet to recognize the time traveler when they meet for the first time at the Residencia (2015: 121).

Fig. 2.3. Ángel Ruiz (left) as Lorca and Rodolfo Sancho as Julián in the
final episode of the first season of TVE's *El Ministerio del Tiempo*

At their final meeting the two men jointly recite Lorca's poem (newly 'imagined' the night before, according to the dialogue), their shared knowledge enhancing an encounter that is sexless but clearly homoerotic. Elsewhere the screenwriters employ their archival research to more daring effect: one female member of the Ministry sleeps with a young woman whose presence at the Residencia is attested by historical sources and is lent her real name in the series (Cruz 2015: 120).

As we have seen, then, in *El Ministerio del Tiempo* the grand narrative of national history is coupled with the small personal chronicles that bear the emotional weight of the series. In the final revelation that is so moving, we discover, also in the climactic Lorca episode, that Julián has by traveling to the past unwittingly caused the accidental death of the wife for whom he has been mourning throughout the season. There are thus losses, both national and individual, that cannot be remedied even by characters gifted with supernatural powers and fully conscious of the weight of historical memory. And nor can the characters (in the series, in history) be healed by the consoling powers of art. Although, as we saw, Julián astonishes Lorca by joining him in reciting one of the latter's as yet unpublished poems (he likely knows it from the famous flamenco version by Camarón de la Isla), he can save neither the poet nor his own wife from tragically early deaths.

This scene is not dissimilar to the one in which Rapún cites a sonnet in *La piedra oscura* that would not be published for some sixty years; or the sequence in *La novia* that is set to a version of Leonard Cohen's much later musical rendering of a poem taken from *Poeta en Nueva York* [Poet in New York]. And the sequence in *El Ministerio del Tiempo* is also a third example (after *La piedra oscura* and *La novia*) of a bracketed or abstracted homoerotic interaction between two men, one likely to strike a chord in Spanish audiences already primed to respond to the question of historical memory and to Lorca's received status as gay martyr.

## Displacement, Revision, Anachronism

We have seen, then, that my three recent texts invoke three different strategies in their engagement with the past: queer displacement, feminist revision, and heuristic anachronism. And they expand and intensify the trend of conspicuous absence that we saw via Alberto Mira in three texts from earlier decades. *La piedra oscura* does not represent the poet directly but rather substitutes for him a homosocial dialogue between young men that projects proleptically into the future of the theater spectators. (An actor playing Lorca was, however, a spectral presence on stage through much of the Mexican production of the play). *La novia* repeats some traditionalist tropes of Lorcan dramaturgy (those stallions and moons) but places its new female protagonist in a new feminine context, thus connecting with the modern cinema audience. Finally, *El Ministerio del Tiempo* juxtaposes past and present (an iPad in a Dalí painting, a liberal time traveler in an illiberal time) in order to prompt viewers to discover for themselves the charge, social and affective, that a historical legacy engages still in contemporary society.

The difference is, of course, that while the play was staged in a prestigious but tiny theater in Madrid and the film sputtered at the Spanish box office, the TV series played on national broadcast television in the homes of an audience of millions, many of whom went on to create fan fictions and art that testify to the intensity of their viewing experience. Despite these differences in audience scale, however, displacement, revision, and anachronism are, finally, three strategies for a new engagement with memory for new audiences in Spain and beyond, provoked by the endlessly productive and seductive figure of Lorca himself.

## References: Text

CASCAJOSA VIRINO, CONCEPCIÓN (ed.). 2015. *Dentro de El Ministerio del Tiempo* (Madrid: Léeme)

CASTILLO HINOJOSA, ANA MARÍA. 2012. 'Ficción audiovisual en redes sociales en línea', *Revista Comunicación*, 10.1: 907–16

COLMEIRO, JOSÉ. 2018. 'Unraveling Memories in Spain', *Journal of Spanish Cultural Studies*, 19: 481–90

CONEJERO, ALBERTO. 2016. *La piedra oscura*, prologue by Ian Gibson (Madrid: Antígona)

CRUZ, YOLANDA. 2015. 'Teatro, cine, y versos al servicio del Ministerio: entre la realidad y el sueño en "La leyenda del tiempo"', in Cascajosa Virino (ed.), pp. 115–22

DELGADO, MARÍA M. 2008. *Federico García Lorca* (London and New York: Routledge)

GARCÍA, ROCÍO. 2015. 'Encuentro con el enemigo', *El País,* 12 January <https://elpais.com/cultura/2015/01/07/babelia/1420649841_006592.html> [accessed 11 February 2021]

GONZÁLEZ CAMAÑO, ÓSCAR. 2015. 'La mirada desde la historia: ¿cualquier tiempo pasado fue mejor?', in Cascajosa Virino (ed.), pp. 59–66

LABANYI, JO. 2008. 'The Politics of Memory in Contemporary Spain', *Journal of Spanish Cultural Studies*, 9: 119–25

LODGE, GUY. 2015. 'Film Review: The Bride', *Variety*, 16 November <https://variety.com/2015/film/festivals/the-bride-review-1201641634/> [accessed 10 February 2021]

MIRA, ALBERTO. 2007. 'Lorca in Cinema', in *A Companion to Federico García Lorca*, ed. by Federico Bonaddio (London: Tamesis/Boydell & Brewer), pp. 122–28

MORA GASPAR, VÍCTOR. 2015. 'Historia y memoria, huellas y signos: imágenes temporales para la construcción de la identidad', in Cascajosa Virino (ed.), pp. 77–84

OCAÑA, JAVIER. 2015. 'Lorca de diseño', *El País*, 10 December <https://elpais.com/cultura/2015/12/10/actualidad/1449758738_718802.html> [accessed 11 February 2021]

## References: Audiovisual

*Amar en tiempos revueltos*. 2005–present. (Diagonal/RTVE)

*A un dios desconocido*. 1977. Dir. by Jaime Chávarri (Elías Querejeta P.C.)

*The Disappearance of García Lorca*. 1997. Dir. by Marcos Zurinaga. (Antena 3/Canal+/ Enrique Cerezo Producciones Cinematográficas)

KO-Z Producciones. 2020. '*La piedra oscura* de Alberto Conejero (México) Teatro', 23 March <https://www.youtube.com/watch?v=ESKTGosdgJI> [accessed 1 March 2021]

*Lorca, muerte de un poeta*. 1987. Dir. by Juan Antonio Bardem (Acción/RAI/TVE)

*Ministerio del Tiempo, El*. 2015–20. (Cliffhanger/RTVE)

*novia, La*. 2015. Dir. by Paula Ortiz (Get In The Picture Productions/TVE)

PART II

# TV Period Pieces

# CHAPTER 3

# Two Televisual *Guernicas*:
# *Genius: Picasso* and
# *El Ministerio del Tiempo*

## Presentism, Feminism, Transmedia

I begin with two primal scenes. In the first, Picasso gleefully begins to paint *Guernica*, inspired by his two female lovers who fight in the studio behind him. In the second, three colleagues and friends, two male and one female, gaze in wonder at and comment admiringly on Picasso's masterpiece in Madrid's Museo Nacional Centro de Arte Reina Sofía [Queen Sofía Art Museum]. The two moments are emblematic of the production and reception of the painting, respectively. And they feature at the end of episodes in two major television series, one American and one Spanish.

In this third chapter, my first on TV period pieces, I treat Picasso as a televisual figure in the USA and Spain in the two very different texts from which my opening examples are taken. The first is *Genius: Picasso* (National Geographic, 2018), an anthology miniseries from basic cable station National Geographic that premiered in the US in June 2018; and the second is the prize-winning science fiction series *El Ministerio del Tiempo* [The Ministry of Time] (RTVE, 2015–20), whose first season of four (which contains an episode focused on the transfer of *Guernica* from New York to Madrid) was first broadcast by public free-to-air channel RTVE in 2015 (see Cascajosa Virino 2015). (This is the same series and season which dedicated the episode to Federico García Lorca that I examined in the previous chapter.)

Both of these TV dramas stage disruptions in place and time. Briefly to anticipate, the disruption in place concerns the much-studied topic of the transnational and the circulation between territories, inspired perhaps by the peregrinations of *Guernica* itself. In this context I will argue further that the foreign-language accent (of actor, of character) serves as a verbal bridge between territories and cultures.

The disruption in time concerns not the transnational but the trans-temporal, bridging periods that are of course normally kept chronologically apart. Both series thus reveal the trace of the past in present, as is conventional in period drama, but also, paradoxically, the trace of the present in the past. Indeed the goal of the characters in the Spanish series is explicitly that of preserving the (dramatic, traumatic) past so that the democratic present may remain the same.

Both series are made necessarily within the constraints of a specific genre, whose current characteristics I will briefly explore. *Genius: Picasso* is the successor to the previous edition of the series, the Emmy-nominated *Genius: Einstein* (2017), which is set in the same historical period, treats the same anti-Fascist theme, and was made by the same creative team. *Picasso* is of course a biographical series that draws on the lengthy film tradition of the biopic. *El Ministerio del Tiempo* is an example of sci-fi/fantasy, a genre little practiced in Spain, but one which in this case also shades into biopic, especially in the final episode of the first series that focuses in unusual depth on the young García Lorca.

The two recent series clearly confirm the continuing interest for both the painter and the painting in many media since its creation. Elena Cueto Asín (2015) has given a full and definitive account of the reception of *Guernica* on stage, page, and screen over some eighty years, covering the three periods of the Civil War, the Franco dictatorship, and the democratic era. Cueto Asín focuses in her huge corpus on the three themes of event, memory, and heritage, and includes coverage of film and television in different genres before my own texts.

Very recent articles on *Guernica* written by scholars in different disciplines reveal the breadth of the fascination for Picasso's painting. In 'Publicizing Atrocity and Legitimizing Outrage: Picasso's *Guernica*' (2018) Jordi Xifra and Robert L. Heath approach the painting from a perspective that may well shock humanists: public relations. Their aim is 'to examine whether and how visual communication can publicize and frame a military event'; and they propose that 'art can contribute impact to public relations efforts, by focusing attention, making issues public, and making informative, framing, and democratizing statements' (2018: 28). This is clearly an instrumental, presentist goal comparable, as we shall see, to the intent of biopic creators.

Almost literally worlds away from this approach is Alister Wedderburn's 'The Reappropriation of an Icon: *Guernica*, Remade' (2019). Wedderburn treats the work of a women's community organization in South Africa which consisted of weaving a tapestry based on Picasso's painting, 'applying it to the group's experience of the ongoing AIDS epidemic' (2019: 480). Wedderburn suggests that here 'a domestic "feminine" craft takes on the privileged public status of art and/or iconography', asserting both the 'grievability' of African victims of disease and the 'malleability' of a privileged international icon (2019: 480). Openly feminist (indeed published in the *International Feminist Journal of Politics*), Wedderburn's study is also concerned by transmedia in its account of the interweaving of a monumental male oil painting and a humble female tapestry.

A third and final article returns *Guernica* to its national historical context by confronting the painting with evidence also drawn from a different medium, namely rare and neglected archival and printed text sources. In 'Looking at Picasso's *Guernica* after the Barcelona May Days of 1937: the Transgressive "Left" and the End of History' (2018), Eugenia Afinoguénova treats the vexed question of the painting's specificity or in Wedderburn's word 'malleability'. Asking if it was 'just about the bombing of Gernika', Afinoguénova argues that the artwork must be placed in the context of writing by poets, publishers, and critics, amongst others, who followed the 'Civil War within the Civil War' between the Catalan government and the anarchists and between the anarchists and Soviet-led Communists (319). Both the genesis and the early interpretation of the painting are thus steeped in the literate culture (of newspapers and journals, letters and postcards) through which Picasso's circle or milieu communicated.

Scholars have identified the same three themes mentioned above in relation to the particular topic of *Guernica* in general accounts of the recent Anglo-American biopic. Taken together these trends suggest that this is no longer, as is still generally thought, a conservative genre, relying on national heritage and a perceived fidelity to past. And although this scholarly literature is primarily devoted to film, much of it holds true for television, given the industrial and aesthetic convergence between the two media.

First, then, current biopic is presentist, not simply recreating the past but appealing with greater or lesser explicitness to issues that are held deeply to concern the contemporary audience for whom it is made (Brown and Vidal 2013: 2). Secondly, it is feminist (or at least post-feminist), addressing the female spectator who seeks active women protagonists, in whatever historical period and whatever the subjection of women at the time in which the series is set (Polaschek 2013). And thirdly the biopic invokes transmedia, not only in its distribution (the already mentioned convergence of film, TV, and internet) but in its story space, frequently focusing as it does on creative figures, including celebrities, who work in varied artistic media (Minier and Pennacchia 2014).

Complementarily, one recent tendency in TV sci-fi/fantasy has been time travel. In the USA no fewer than three titles with this premise were premiered in the 2016 season. As we shall see, one of these (NBC's *Timeless*) has a special and disputed connection with *El Ministerio del Tiempo*. While the time travel subgenre clearly testifies to a newly intense interest in the bodily experience of the past, it also puts into play a less transparent convention, namely that a period that appears to have little in common with the present (whether past or future) has uncanny parallels with it. As we shall see once more, some commentators on the *Picasso* series make somewhat problematic connections between the rise of Fascism in the 1930s and current political conditions in the USA. Likewise the Civil War is presented by characters within *El Ministerio del Tiempo* as just the latest and most vicious in a series of bloody fratricidal conflicts that mark and mar the history of Spain.

More generally, and as is well known, the TV medium is currently in a state of flux around the world. Once television was considered domestic (consumed within the home), female (directed above all to the women viewers who also favor period drama), and everyday (integrated into the rhythm of daily life (Spigel and Mann 1992)). These characteristics could hardly be further from the cult of 'genius' celebrated by National Geographic. The latter appeals to a Kantian aesthetic attitude to a work of art that is held to be unique, one that, ironically enough, has recently been taken up by television scholars (Peacock and Jacobs 2013). And in the series itself Picasso is shot repeatedly from a low angle, looming heroically over camera and viewer as he grapples with the canvas. Choices in shooting style thus reinforce ideological positioning.

Fig. 3.1. Antonio Banderas as the older Picasso in
National Geographic's miniseries *Genius: Picasso*

## Questions of Quality

In the last twenty years so-called quality or 'complex' TV (Mittell 2015) has
dominated premium cable and streaming platforms in the USA and beyond. Unlike
the domesticated broadcast television, this new medium is founded on 'difficult
men' (as both showrunners and protagonists (Brett 2013)), a lineage within which
Picasso clearly takes up a privileged position. Indeed the series *Picasso* was explicitly
described at its US premiere as 'quality TV' by Antonio Banderas himself, the star
who plays the older version of the artist in it (Grobar 2018).

Likewise the little-known American actor who plays the young Picasso (Alex
Rich) made a connection at the same event between the *National Geographic*
magazine's distinguished history of still photography and the series' evocative and
highly crafted cinematography. While there is a conflict between US definitions
of quality as boundary-pushing and edgy content and European understanding of
the term as one based on cultural heritage and distinction (a difference ably treated
by the major theorist of global television genres in Europe and the USA, Milly
Buonanno (1998, 2014)), the volatile label of 'quality' clearly brings with it material
effects in both production and distribution.

Within the still ceaseless flow of mainstream TV scheduling, then, both series
treated here count as event or marquee programming with transnational ambitions.
The second season of *Genius* was thus local and global in its aspirations. The world
premiere was held in Málaga on 22 March 2018, an event and location for which
Banderas took the credit. His shared birthplace with the painter was also invoked

as a supposed special connection between the two international Spanish figures. Addressing the local press Banderas had said explicitly once more that Picasso 'es de mi tierra' [he is from my land], 'este personaje me puede llegar a la gloria o me pueden echar de Málaga' [this character could either make my name or get me thrown out of Málaga] (the latter comment was actually made on the prospect of a film biopic by Carlos Saura that was never produced, more evidence for the convergence of cinema and television) (Víctor Gómez 2017, 2018). The fact that the US premiere of the series was at the Tribeca Film Festival in New York City one month later, on 21 April, also confirmed quality television's aspiration to appropriate the perhaps threatened prestige of transnational art cinema.

Likewise *El Ministerio del Tiempo* was a rare critical success for RTVE, which, like the National Geographic channel which had previously specialized in worthy documentaries, was not known for such adventurous titles. The Spanish series won international prizes in countries such as Mexico, where it earned the Platino award for the significantly titled 'Best Ibero-American Series' (Inma Gómez 2018). Given that Spanish series generally elicit relatively little interest in Latin America, it would appear, then, that in this unique case Spanish history could be re-inscribed in a broader Hispano-American context.

Meanwhile the showrunner of *El Ministerio del Tiempo* is one of the few in Spain comparable to the more celebrated 'difficult men' of the US: Javier Olivares, with his now deceased brother Pablo, already boasted a distinguished track record in period drama for the Spanish state broadcaster with *Isabel* (RTVE, 2011–14 (on the medieval Catholic queen)) and *Víctor Ros* (RTVE, 2014–15 (on a nineteenth-century detective)), both produced by the brothers' independent production company Cliffhanger. The fact that the male lead of *Isabel* would reappear in *El Ministerio del Tiempo* (Rodolfo Sancho, who had played Fernando el Católico, was indisputably the biggest star of this second series) also suggests an auteurist continuity between Olivares' high profile projects.

The concept of 'genius' as unique and isolated coincides with the TV genre of the mini- or limited series which serves as a positional good for transnational audiovisual circulation. It does so in part by appealing to movie stars (Banderas as Picasso, previously Geoffrey Rush as Einstein) and the lush, meticulously recreated period *mise en scène*, shared by both series. Rodolfo Sancho was also television royalty in Spain, as audiences were well aware that he was the son of Sancho Gracia, the star of *Curro Jiménez* (1976–79), a classic and much-loved period series of the Transition to democracy. Conversely, then, just as quality television sets itself apart from ordinary (domestic) TV, so genius isolates itself from history and politics.

Such hermetic isolation can be called into question, however, by the demands of the present. For example the problem of Picasso's misogyny has become newly current, especially for the quality female audience to which period TV drama is mainly directed. One typical article in *Elle* (Doyle 2016), before the series was screened, compares Picasso's abusive treatment of his lovers Dora Maar and Francoise Gilot to that of later artists in film who exhibited troubling behavior towards female collaborators (Hitchcock and Bertolucci). The Spanish painter is thus inserted into current controversies over the power that prominent men can wield over dependent women in the cultural sphere.

Responding to such debates in its negative review of the series (Fienberg 2018), *Hollywood Reporter* laments that in the age of #MeToo women's screams are relegated to the background of a male life story (in the very first scene we hear the future artist's mother in childbirth, but the focus is on his father and uncle). And the writer claims that the innovative artwork of *Guernica* is reduced, as mentioned earlier, to a catfight between two of the painters' many mistresses, Marie-Thérèse Walter, the mother of his first child, and photographer Dora Maar (Fienberg 2018).

### *Genius: Picasso*: Biography Against History

In spite of these negative portrayals of its subject and of the series itself, *Genius: Picasso* coincides to some extent with the recent positive trends in biopic sketched earlier. The series is clearly presentist. Thus the *Variety* review (O'Keefe 2018), more positive than that of rival *Hollywood Reporter*, claims that the drama's urgent requirement to take up a political position (as when Picasso is repeatedly requested to paint a picture protesting political violence) parallels the present situation in the USA where cultural producers are under pressure to be, in the ubiquitous neologism, 'woke'. It is no accident, then, that there is an anachronistic rock guitar playing on the trailer soundtrack. And that the tagline for the series should be aggressively demotic, branding the great man 'a piece of work'.

Mindful of the current cultural climate in which it was produced, the *Picasso* series also strives intermittently to be feminist. Throughout, the womanizer is shown to have some respect for his mistresses, thus connecting with the series' target female audience. One late episode suggests that the painter still cares for his now elderly ex-partner Marie-Thérèse Walter (and indeed for his lifelong gay Jewish friend Max Jacob). He is also shown to considerably delay an affair with a young and inexperienced admirer who is presented as overeager to become his latest lover.

Finally, the series is very transmedia in its ambitions, and not only in its necessary focus on painting in all Picasso's varied periods. Unsurprisingly, there is an explicit synergy between the TV drama and the veteran print magazine, which was made accessible online. In the special issue of *National Geographic* celebrating the series' premiere (May 2018), Picasso is called, in a contradictory mix of adjectives, 'intense, provocative, disturbing, captivating'. The main magazine article (Kalb 2018) is also varied, celebrating in turn genealogy or heritage (via an interview with Picasso's grandson, Olivier Widmeier Picasso), but also renewed innovation (via an interview with a young female artist, Allison Zukerman, who re-appropriates Picasso's work). Connecting with the educational ambitions of the very different and more skeptical and ironic *El Ministerio del Tiempo*, the magazine also insists on pedagogy: in a large-format photo small Spanish children dressed in colorful coats are shown sitting on the floor at the Reina Sofía before the famously monochrome painting. It is the very image of a now vibrant and youthful democratic Spain founded in Picasso's historic artistic creation.

The main innovation of the miniseries itself is that its plot, rejecting the Bildungsroman format traditional in the genre, is not linear. From the start there are constant and disorientating jumps in time, in scenes alternating between the two actors playing the subject, Banderas and Rich. It is here that the question of accent is of the essence. *Hollywood Reporter* invokes the term as a derisive name for mannered school of period acting when it cites 'bizarre accent and performance choices' (Fienberg 2018). And the genre is even capitalized as 'Bad Accent Theater'. This is the linguistic equivalent, perhaps, of the clichéd dialogue ('I want to do something original. Unique!') and of the reduction of women to mere muses who inspire exceptional men, according to the industry journal's negative reaction to the series.

But Banderas himself, a living bridge between Spain and the USA, is more ambivalent about the role of the accent. In a major and sympathetic interview for the *New York Times*, timed to promote the series' release on 18 April 2018, he notes with admirable self-awareness how his non-native English had proved both positive and negative for his career in US, where he embodied a persistent source of anxiety as a Spanish-speaker in an English-language industry (Brodesser-Akner 2018).

On the one hand Banderas says that he was denied the possibility of taking standard leading US roles (examples he cites are bankers or astronauts). But on the other he was encouraged, beyond Hispanic or 'Latino' clichés, to take on marginal, transgressive character choices, beginning with the gay lover of protagonist Tom Hanks in the early AIDS drama *Philadelphia* (Jonathan Demme, 1993). As the journalist writes, while Banderas's characters for Almodóvar in Spain already came with a soul, his sometimes stereotypical Latin roles in the US required him actively to create that inner life. This transnational relation is encoded in the TV text of *Genius: Picasso*, but not of course made explicit in its narrative, via the pervasive presence of non-native English language voiced or reproduced by the entire cast. But it is more productively set in play by the now lengthy and inescapable star profile of Banderas as a bridge between Spain and the USA, between Europe and the Americas.

Let us turn now to the first episode of the series *Genius: Picasso*. It begins, as mentioned earlier, with a spectacular birth: the apparently dead baby Picasso is revived when blown by a male relative with tobacco smoke. Later, in what are presented as privileged moments, the subject is taken as a small child to a bullfight, where he is enraptured by images of vital danger; and loses his virginity as a teenager in a brothel, thus establishing the artist's pecuniary relation to a first female muse (after the sex act, he asks to sketch the prostitute). It would be difficult to imagine scenes less sympathetic to a contemporary Anglo-American female audience, likely to be hostile to both Spain's national fiesta and men's patronage of sex workers.

Yet the young Picasso is also portrayed as caring towards women: he is tender towards his short-lived younger sister; and, in a disorientating time jump, is shown as a loving if intermittent father to an infant daughter who is herself shown painting. Moreover, in the older Picasso's scenes with Dora Maar, the latter is consistently shown as a creator herself, always busy with her camera. Beyond mere muse, Maar is also presented as the true political instigator of *Guernica*. It is she who reads aloud a newspaper account of the outrage, as the series uses its evidently high budget to convincingly recreate the devastating bombing of the town and the merciless strafing of the civilian victims outside it.

The climax of the opening episode shows the creation of the great painting to be not only, as critics feared, a fight between the two rival women. In a short but significant sequence, the episode employs a unique technique, demonstrating that *Guernica* is a privileged moment in both the life and the life story. We are given quick-cut analytic montage, an alternation between monochrome and color, and the juxtaposition of both the recreation of the recent historic event (the military atrocity) and the memory of distant personal incidents (the bull and horse from the *corrida* seen as young child; also the long dead sister). Showy high and low angles are also more frequent here than elsewhere. Generally in the series, artistic innovation is announced in declamatory dialogue ('I cannot follow rules and models!'). Here, uniquely, radical creativity is reenacted in the shooting and cutting style: the TV technique employed is a fitting analogue for a classic moment of artistic experimentation, but only here in the case of *Guernica*.

### *El Ministerio del Tiempo*: Ordinary Genius

Let us turn or return now in contrast to *El Ministerio del Tiempo*. As a time travel series it incorporates the disjunctions of time and space offered by national history into the domestic, everyday life of the TV medium and hence of Spanish viewers. And as an example of quality programming from the state broadcaster (of prize-winning prestige), it derives its cultural distinction from fidelity to the past once more. It is no accident that the episode's lengthy 'making of' stresses the authenticity of the series' image and sound design (RTVE 2015a).

Here, as in *Picasso*, artistic ambition in television is also imbued with painting. In the only academic article on the subject of the series' relation to art, included in Concepción Cascajosa's excellent book on the series, Mónica Barrientos-Bueno notes (2015: 165) that as early as the opening scene of the first episode, set in a battlefield in Flanders, there is a reference to Velázquez's history painting called alternately *La rendición de Breda* or *Las lanzas* [The Surrender of Breda, The Lances]. In that same opening episode, the modern-day character also stumbles across the palace chamber in which *Las Meninas* is about to be painted. The fifth episode, the one focusing on *Guernica*, culminates with a meeting between Velázquez and Picasso that stages a kind of circle of consecration between past and present, but also between painting and television.

The series' fidelity to history (achieved in part via citations of old master painting) is uniquely combined with a canny digital address to viewers, exploiting social media in a way unprecedented on Spanish television and aiming to engage with what Natalia Marcos, *El País*'s senior TV reviewer, has called 'the Twitter generation' (2015). Moreover spin-off videos still posted on TVE's website confer historical legitimation on the series via the internet. Rosario Peiró, whose position is given as 'Directora de la colección, Museo Reina Sofía' [Director of the

Collection, Queen Sofía Museum], presented her pioneering scholarly internet project on *Guernica* (2018) at the day conference 'El *Guernica* como puente cultural entre España y los EEUU' [*Guernica* as a Cultural Bridge between Spain and the USA]. This event, at which I also presented, was held at the Madrid headquarters of the Instituto Cervantes and organized by the Universidad Rey Juan Carlos and the Fundación Consejo España–EEUU on 5 July 2018. Peiró also lent her expert specialist commentary to one of the promotional videos for the television series (RTVE 2015b).

With *El Ministerio del Tiempo*, traditional biopic TV is here not just feminine but also explicitly feminist: old macho Spain (the sixteenth-century soldier Alonso de Entrerríos, played by Nacho Fresneda) is confronted with a new female order in which one woman (the nineteenth-century student Amelia Folch (Aura Garrido)) is the team leader and another (a senior functionary of the ministry, Irene Larra Girón (Cayetana Guillén Cuervo)) has a wife. The modern man (Julián Martínez, the caring paramedic still grieving for his deceased wife (Rodolfo Sancho)), is shown clearing the table after the team's dinner, to the evident surprise of the Golden Age military officer.

The series' gender pedagogy is paralleled by its explicit dialogue on the meaning of the journey of the painting from New York to Madrid. At different points in the episode characters suggest that *Guernica*'s 'return' (in fact it had never before been in the country) represents the coming of democracy to Spain and the reconciliation of two Spains. While these two morals are not quite the same thing, of course, they serve a common purpose of educating contemporary audiences on the roles perceived to be played by the painting in the 1980s and beyond.

Beyond historical fact, the relationship between Spain and the US is surprisingly troubling, as presented here in the series' sci-fi context. The McGuffin of the episode is the bill of sale which Picasso is said to have received from the Republican Government and which proves Spanish ownership of the picture, a document which the Ministry repeatedly fails to find. The agents' first failed attempt is in a Barcelona hotel during an air raid in 1939; its second at the Madrid airport in 1981, when the painting itself is due to arrive. The villain here is an American time traveler said to be employed by New York's Museum of Modern Art in its effort to hold on to the picture by changing the past. Actor Jimmy Shaw, who plays the antagonist called Walcott, serves as a rare Spanish-speaking bridge between US and Spain. Known for his television work in both countries, he might be seen as a small-scale and inverted version of Banderas' grander 'actor with an accent'.

Walcott claims dismissively at one point, in Shaw's accented but correct Castilian, that Spaniards remain obsessed with the glories of the past, unlike, we presume, present-focused North Americans like himself. But, as the plot develops, he is kidnapped and tricked by the Spanish functionaries. We might compare the previous episode (number 4) where a New York Jewish lawyer attempts unsuccessfully to retrieve the *Book of Doors* that is said to be the origin of the Ministry and was originally given to Isabel la Católica by a rabbi threatened with burning at the stake by the Inquisition (in a typically meticulous attention to detail,

Fig. 3.2. Raúl Pulido as the young Picasso in an episode of
TVE's series *El Ministerio del Tiempo*

we are given a close-up of the original title in Hebrew script: 'Sefer Dlatot'). Finally the threatened book (as, later, the threatened painting) remains in Madrid.

The series thus stages a certain anxiety about the threats of American technology and cultural appropriation, even positing a relation of rivalry of the once global empire with the current superpower. It is perhaps no accident that the makers of *El Ministerio del Tiempo*, who had pitched a remake of their creation in the USA, mounted a lawsuit against American network NBC when it subsequently launched its own time travel series *Timeless* (2016–18). The latter boasted the same premise of preserving the national past (albeit a much shorter one in the case of the United States than that of Spain) and the same team of two guys and a girl. The case was finally settled out of court in favor of the Spanish producer Cliffhanger and its CEO Olivares (Anonymous 2017).

This episode of the successful arrival of *Guernica* can be read, then, in part as a fantasy of revenge on US technological superiority and global influence. But in general, *El Ministerio del Tiempo* is hardly nationalist; rather it serves as an affectionate satire on the Spanish national project. In this episode the team finally fake the document they have failed to find, using a signature they have procured from the young Picasso, a strategy that is declared by one character to be 'very Spanish'. The 'picaresque' tradition of knavery is also invoked in the dialogue here. And the next episode, number 6, will feature the original fictional *pícaro*, Lazarillo de Tormes, presented here as a historical figure.

In spite of the successful transfer of *Guernica* in this episode, the first season of the series often focuses, as we saw in the previous chapter, on national humiliations, not triumphs: the Peninsular War, whose hero Juan Martín Díez 'El Empecinado' [The Stubborn One] was subsequently executed (episode 1); Felipe II's Armada, which proved not so invincible (the team's aim is typically not to reverse the historical disaster but to save a young and womanizing Lope de Vega from premature drowning) (episode 2); and the mediocre reign of Isabel II, which would end in Revolution, abdication, and exile (episode 7).

Most affecting and relevant for the case of Picasso and *Guernica*, however, is the integration of 'genius' and the transcendent work of art into everyday life through parallel plotlines. The arrival of the painting in Madrid in 1981 is matched in the episode by the modern character Julián's return to that same place and time, where he unexpectedly witnesses his own father's affair with another woman. The episode also demonstrates the democratization of culture in modern Spain, as the *movida madrileña* is recreated with as much respect as the Madrid of Picasso's early years. Indeed this is a parallel made explicit in the dialogue which references the dusty yet invigorating capital in the two periods. The 'making of' on TVE's website (characteristically dignified here with the pseudo-academic name 'archivos' [archives]) resorts to the documentary conventions of period footage and authoritative voice-over on only two occasions: to explain the historical tragedy of Guernica and the more recent cultural renaissance of the *movida*.

The case of the painting is solved only when Velázquez, lightly disguised, meets Picasso in a picturesque Madrid bar in 1899 and asks for the autograph that will be used by the Ministry to fake the bill of sale. In lengthy dialogue, each proclaims the other the greatest of Spanish artists, with *Las Meninas* serving as a precedent for Picasso's as yet uncreated large-scale masterpiece. It is striking that the young Picasso is depicted in this episode as handsome, modest, and sympathetic, far from the notoriously misogynist macho who is decried elsewhere. And just as avant-garde painting is in this sequence legitimated by an old master, so the new genre of quality or complex TV is consecrated by repeated appeal to and incorporation of the traditional medium of fine art.

In the last scene of the episode the whole team gathers to view the painting (this is an expert digital effect, as the crew could not film in the Reina Sofía itself). *Guernica* is shown only now, having been withheld throughout the running time. And at this climax even the sixteenth-century soldier, previously dismissive of Picasso's works as childish daubing, is now reconciled to his brilliance. The theme of Spanish 'genius' returns here in some triumph. But a tone of ambivalence and melancholy remain pervasive because of the other plotlines in this fifth episode of the first season: the disturbing revelation of the specially inhuman cruelty of twentieth-century war to the characters from earlier periods who cannot conceive of such mass inhumanity; and the modern paramedic's realization that it was an unknown woman, not his mother, who was the true love of his father's life.

Fidelity, a key term in the biopic and period genres, is thus difficult to define, in either artistic or personal terms. In striking contrast to his father's mobile affections, it is Rodolfo Sancho's faithful paramedic once more who confesses to his colleagues, as they stand mesmerized in front of *Guernica*, that it was the dead wife, to whom he remains fiercely loyal, who had explained to him the meaning of the picture.

Actor Aura Garrido, the female lead in *El Ministerio del Tiempo*, suggests in interview in the 'making of' cited earlier that time in her series is not linear but parallel. Likewise the constant temporal jumps in *Picasso*, go beyond conventional flashbacks or forwards, perhaps in an attempt to invoke *Guernica*'s simultaneity of action, frozen on the canvas but ever renewed in its modernity. Now, it seems, Picasso's biography must, signaling presentism, be set to the soundtrack of a rock guitar and embodied by an actor (Banderas) who is forever associated, even in the USA, with the *movida madrileña* and its creator Almodóvar, a figure who could hardly be more different from Picasso.

## Heritage, Memory, Institution

Elena Cueto Asín, the author of an encyclopedic monograph on *Guernica*'s afterlives, later dedicated an article to the *El Ministerio del Tiempo* episode I treat here (2019). Like her book, the article focuses on heritage and memory (here more precisely 'institutional memory'). Much of the article reviews the discursive precursors to the series during the Transition to democracy: the press coverage in 1981 in print and on television of the painting's 'return' to Spain (2019: 239); and the perhaps surprising 'ironic intellectual posture' of newspaper columnists such as the Francisco Umbral and lesser-known experimental playwrights (2019: 242). More extreme were the 'diatribe' by artist Antonio Saura, attacking the government's culture policy which, he claimed, had turned art into a 'commodity'; and a novel that posited the theft of *Guernica* in New York by ETA and its substitution by a fake in Madrid (2019: 243) (we have seen the officers of the Ministerio del Tiempo are also not averse to faking documents).

Of course the mass media, more than these maverick creators, have more power to produce 'official memory', the role taken upon itself after the Dictatorship by public Televisión Española (2019: 244). And for Cueto, *El Ministerio del Tiempo* continues this 'hegemonic discourse' of celebrating the 'achievements' of the newly democratic Spanish state (246). Yet, she admits, the series' presentation of the picture's transfer to Spain is by no means 'epic'. Rather the episode displays a certain 'emotional distance' and 'cold acceptance of the instrumental function' of the picture, which is to serve as a symbol of the 'reconciliation of the two Spains after the Dictatorship'. It is an aim announced without fanfare (2019: 247).

I would contest Cueto Asín's stress on the dispassionate nature of the episode (for me the grand heritage narrative is interwoven with a plotline of intimate human passion from which it is difficult to disentangle). But I would agree with her contention that *El Ministerio del Tiempo*'s presentation of the art work and its journey to Madrid is no longer 'epic', but rather taken for granted, already known. Cueto Asín begins her article by noting that when Julián's boss tells him solemnly of the national and historical value of the painting as symbol, he replies quite casually: 'Lo sé' [I know] (2019: 238).

The final paradox, then, is that the unique achievement of 'genius', self-removed from the demands of daily life, should be best caught by the medium of television, which, in spite of the recent rise of quality or complex TV, is traditionally held to be domestic, everyday, and repetitive. But although both aspire to cultural distinction, the two series make very different uses of *Guernica*. In *Genius: Picasso*, in spite of gestures towards political engagement and feminist consciousness, the personal threatens nonetheless to distract from and trivialize the political: as we saw, the rival mistresses physically fight as Picasso paints his masterpiece. It is a sequence that suggests, most problematically, that it is this small biographical detail, rather than the large historical tragedy, that is the true motive of Picasso's masterpiece.

In *El Ministerio del Tiempo*, on the other hand, the personal is intimately integrated into the political, as the team finally views a picture that is presented as the image of a democratic Spain in which, as we see throughout the series, women's rights are held to be central. Typically also, in the very last shot, the three protagonists' heads, shown from behind, are rapidly hidden by those of other anonymous viewers of the picture, suggesting a collective and democratic access to culture that goes beyond the individual and personal.

In spite of the seriousness of this episode's conclusion, the Spanish series generally has a sense of self-deprecating humor and irony that the high seriousness of the American drama, announced by its very title, cannot permit itself. We have seen that National Geographic's *Genius: Picasso*, true to that title, offers an individualist view of artistic creation in which the personal takes precedence over the political and, that conversely, RTVE's *El Ministerio del Tiempo* integrates the aesthetic object and its creator into the lived experience of the nation and its viewers, preserving and reframing the social dimension of the original work of art. However, the temporal leaps of *Genius: Picasso* and the gates of *El Ministerio del Tiempo* still stand finally as evocative bridges in time and space built in the borderlands between the twin media of painting and television and the two nations of Spain and the USA.

## References: Text

AFINOGUÉNOVA, EUGENIA. 2018. 'Looking at Picasso's *Guernica* after the Barcelona May Days of 1937: the Transgressive "Left" and the End of History', *Journal of Spanish Cultural Studies*, 19.3: 319–38

ANONYMOUS. 2017. 'El litigio por plagio entre *El Ministerio del Tiempo y Timeless* se cierra con un acuerdo', *El País*, 26 May <https://elpais.com/cultura/2017/05/26/television/1495815360_931932.html> [accessed 19 July 2018]

BARRIENTOS-BUENO, MÓNICA. 2015. 'Velázquez y lo pictórico a ambos lados de las puertas del tiempo', in *Dentro de 'El Ministerio del Tiempo'*, ed. by Concepción Cascajosa Virino (Madrid: Léeme), pp. 165–77

BRODESSER-AKNER, TAFFY. 2018. 'Antonio Banderas Doesn't Think You'll Remember Him. Not Yet', *New York Times*, 18 April <https://www.nytimes.com/2018/04/18/arts/antonio-banderas-genius-picasso.html> [accessed 19 July 2018]

BROWN, TOM, and BELÉN VIDAL (eds). 2013. *The Biopic in Contemporary Film Culture* (London: Routledge)

BUONANNO, MILLY. 1998. *The Age of Television: Experiences and Theories* (Bristol: Intellect)

——. 2014. 'Quality Television and Transnational Standards', lecture given at Graduate Center, City University of New York, 21 November

CASCAJOSA VIRINO, CONCEPCIÓN (ed.). 2015. *Dentro de 'El Ministerio del Tiempo'* (Madrid: Léeme)

Cueto Asín, Elena. 2017. *Guernica en la escena, la página, y la pantalla* (Zaragoza: Prensas de la Universidad de Zaragoza)

—— 2019. '*Guernica* como memoria y patrimonio institucional: *El Ministerio del Tiempo*', in *Historia cultural de la Transición: pensamiento crítico y ficciones en literatura, cine, y televisión*, ed. by Carmen Peña Ardid (Madrid: Catarata), pp. 238–51

Doyle, Sadie. 2016. 'Bertolucci Wasn't the First Man to Abuse a Woman and Call it Art and He Won't Be the Last', *Elle*, 8 December <https://www.elle.com/culture/career-politics/a41293/bertolucci-abuse-art/> [accessed 19 July 2018]

Fienberg, Daniel. 2018. '*Genius: Picasso*: TV Review', *Hollywood Reporter*, 23 April <https://www.hollywoodreporter.com/review/genius-picasso-review-1104722> [accessed 19 July 2018]

Gómez, Inma. 2018. '*El Ministerio del Tiempo* mejor serie en los premios Platino 2018', *Culturamas*, 30 April <http://www.culturamas.es/blog/2018/04/30/el-ministerio-del-tiempo-mejor-serie-en-los-premios-platino-2018/> [accessed 19 July 2018]

Gómez, Víctor A. 2017. 'Y Banderas por fin se citó con Picasso', *La Opinión de Málaga*, 1 November <https://www.laopiniondemalaga.es/cultura-espectaculos/2017/11/01/banderas-cito-picasso/965155.html> [accessed 19 July 2018]

——. 2018. '*Genius: Picasso* tendrá su estreno mundial en el Cervantes', *La Opinión de Málaga*, 13 March <https://www.laopiniondemalaga.es/cultura-espectaculos/2018/03/13/genius-picasso-tendra-estreno-mundial/992763.html> [accessed 19 July 2018]

Grobar, Matt. 2018. 'Why Antonio Banderas Was Reluctant to Portray Iconic Painter for *Genius: Picasso* — Tribeca Studio', *Deadline*, 19 April <https://deadline.com/2018/04/genius-picasso-antonio-banderas-alex-rich-tribeca-interview-news-1202371093/> [accessed 19 July 2018]

Kalb, Claudia. 2018. 'How Picasso's Journey from Prodigy to Icon Revealed a Genius', *National Geographic*, May <https://www.nationalgeographic.com/magazine/2018/05/genius-picasso-creativity-greatness-prodigy-legacy/> [accessed 19 July 2018]

Marcos, Natalia. 2015. 'Una serie para la generación Twitter', in *Dentro de 'El Ministerio del Tiempo'*, ed. by Concepción Cascajosa Virino (Madrid: Léeme), pp. 199–202

Martin, Brett. 2013. *Difficult Men: Behind the Scenes of a Creative Revolution: From 'The Sopranos' and 'The Wire' to 'Mad Men' and 'Breaking Bad'* (New York: Penguin)

Minier, Márta, and Maddalena Pennacchia (eds). 2014 *Adaptation, Intermediality and the British Celebrity Biopic* (Farnham: Ashgate)

Mittell, Jason. 2015. *Complex TV: The Poetics of Contemporary Television Storytelling* (New York: New York University Press)

O'Keefe, Kevin. 2018. 'TV Review: *Genius: Picasso* with Antonio Banderas', *Variety*, 17 April <https://variety.com/2018/tv/reviews/tv-review-genius-picasso-antonio-banderas-1202747541/> [accessed 19 July 2018]

Peacock, Steven, and Jason Jacobs (eds). 2013. *Television Aesthetics and Style* (London and New York: Bloomsbury)

Peiró, Rosario. 2018. 'Repensar *Guernica*' <http://guernica.museoreinasofia.es> [accessed 19 July 2018]

Polaschek, Bronwyn. 2013. *The Post-Feminist Biopic: Narrating the Lives of Plath, Kahlo, Woolf and Austen* (Basingstoke and New York: Palgrave Macmillan)

RTVE. 2015a. 'Los archivos del Ministerio: capítulo 5' <http://www.rtve.es/alacarta/videos/los-archivos-del-ministerio/archivos-del-ministerio-capitulo-5/3058842/> [accessed 19 July 2018]

——. 2015b. 'El Ministerio del Tiempo: El *Guernica* es el primer exiliado de la Guerra Civil' <http://www.rtve.es/alacarta/videos/programa/mdt-guernica-exiliado/3058375/> [accessed 19 July 2018]

Spigel, Lynn, and Denise Mann (eds). 1992. *Private Screenings: Television and the Female Consumer* (Minneapolis and London: University of Minnesota Press)

Wedderburn, Alister. 2019. 'The Reappropriation of an Icon: *Guernica*, Remade', *International Feminist Journal of Politics*, July, 21.3: 480–87

Xifra, Jordi, and Robert L. Heath. 2018. 'Publicizing Atrocity and Legitimizing Outrage: Picasso's *Guernica*', *Public Relations Review*, March, 44.1: 28–36

## References: Audiovisual

*Curro Jiménez*. 1976–79. (RTVE)

*Genius: Einstein*. 2017. (EUE/Sokolow/National Geographic)

*Genius: Picasso*. 2018. (EUE/Sokolow/National Geographic)

*Isabel*. 2011–14. (Cliffhanger/RTVE)

*Ministerio del Tiempo, El*. 2015–20. (Cliffhanger/RTVE)

*Philadelphia*. 1993. Dir. by Jonathan Demme (TriStar Pictures)

*Timeless*. 2016. (Middkid Productions/Kripke Enterprises/NBC)

*Víctor Ros*. 2014–15. (Cliffhanger/RTVE)

# CHAPTER 4

# Fortunata italiana?
## *Sceneggiato*, *Serie Clásica*, and TV Nation Formation

### Dramatic Histories

The 'classic series' or literary adaptation is one of the best known, and most praised and maligned, of European television genres (we examined the key example of the bio-series on García Lorca in Chapter 2). Yet its prevalence across the continent disguises national differences in text and context. This fourth chapter, the second in the 'TV Period Pieces' section, aims to put into dialogue a much loved and studied Spanish example of the genre known as *serie clásica* with the earlier Italian version of historical drama called *sceneggiato*.

While I do not attempt to prove direct influence from one country to another, I intend to provide a new matrix for rereading a familiar text, the adaptation of Benito Pérez Galdós's compendious novel *Fortunata y Jacinta* (1887) which was made into ten leisurely hour-long episodes by film director Mario Camus in 1980, that is, during the Transition to democracy. As we shall see, scholarship around the Italian genre provides a kind of defamiliarizing device for shedding light on the role of TV fiction in nation formation and a new approach to reading the Spanish televisual text.

This question has recently been explored in a rare and pioneering collection of essays on the history of media in the two countries, Eduardo Urios-Aparisi and Giovanni Spani's *Diálogos e influencias: cine y televisión en Italia y en España* [Dialogues and Influences: Film and Television in Italy and Spain] (2020). The title is significant. In their introduction the two editors stress that 'la relación entre cine italiano y español no se puede reducir a temas y estilos' [the relationship between Italian and Spanish cinema cannot be reduced to themes and styles] (2020: 4). Moreover, if 'dialogue' cannot be collapsed into 'influence', the question of nationality is also complex in this context:

> ¿Hasta qué punto se puede considerar una visión de la identidad nacional y las fronteras de relación entre los dos países como un constructo que rechaza la dimensión localista y nacionalista? ¿Dónde y cómo deben analizarse los sistemas de complejas relaciones que a menudo son de carácter supranacional? (2020: 4)

[To what extent can a vision of national identity and the boundaries of relations between two countries be considered a construct that rejects the localist and nationalist dimension? Where and how can we analyze systems of complex relationships which often transcend the national?]

Along these lines Urios-Aparisi and Spani note that while no fewer than three essays in their volume are devoted to the Spanish importation of Italian neorealism (Mario Camus' early feature films, made long before *Fortunata y Jacinta*, are mentioned here) (2020: 3), others address filmic resources like landscape and music, shared themes such as terrorism, and parallel auteurs like Pedro Almodóvar and Paolo Sorrentino (2020: 6–7).

Likewise this chapter of mine is based more on dialogue than influence. Yet there is some modest evidence for Spaniards' awareness of their Italian opposite numbers' prior achievements in historical drama and literary adaptation. For example, as early as 1965, just nine years after regular TV broadcasting began in Spain, in his book *Televisión, un arte nuevo* [Television: A New Art], José María Baget Herms (later a major figure in Catalan TV) praises the pioneering Italian contribution to new trends in the medium. Baget makes a connection with film auteurs, pointedly distinguishing Italy from France in its more 'friendly' attitude to the new medium:

> Hemos hablado de Italia, y justo será recordar su aportación a las corrientes modernas de la TV. Esta ha sido cuantiosa e importante: frente a la indiferencia orgullosa adoptada por algunos directores franceses […], sus colegas italianos han comprendido rápidamente la necesidad de adaptarse a las nuevas técnicas, ante la aparición de un competidor que también puede ser un amigo. (1965: 93)

> [We have mentioned Italy; and it is right to remember that country's contribution to modern trends in television. This has been substantial and important: compared to the proud indifference adopted by some French film directors…, their Italian counterparts have rapidly understood the need to adapt to new techniques in the face of the emergence of a rival that can also serve as a friend.]

Baget goes on to praise Vittorio Gassman and his collaborator Enrico Zardi precisely for their record in transnational historical drama, both literary adaptations (Shakespeare's *Othello*) and period pieces (the French Revolution-set *I giacobini* [The Jacobins]) (1965: 94–95).

Likewise, Manuel Palacio, an enduring commentator on the medium and on *Fortunata* itself, notes as a precedent to the Spanish *series clásicas* RAI's lavish life of Leonardo da Vinci (1971), which was shown (like the BBC's literary adaptation *The Forsyte Saga* (1967)) in a dubbed version on RTVE (2001: 153). But Palacio's main focus as critic of *Fortunata* is as an example of 'pedagogy', that is the way in which Spanish television, in both fiction and non-fiction programming, sought to teach its viewers the rights and responsibilities of democracy.

This Spanish context is later supplemented or complemented by that of Sally Faulkner, the other major and long-lasting critic of the series. Faulkner treats rather the middlebrow, the perilous balance of the series between high and low culture. This approach is more clearly international in focus and, indeed, draws mainly (like subsequent scholars) on Pierre Bourdieu's analysis of cultural distinction in France.

Yet both critics, Palacio and Faulkner, have appealed to this series and this genre as exemplary in a movement from the particular to the general in the study of media and society. And they have shown a continuing and developing interest in the text which varies slightly in focus over time, as shown by their most recent accounts.

My own study of the series (2006: 27–57) added the theme of public service (most closely associated in TV studies with the UK and the BBC) to those of literarity and the middlebrow, familiar from Faulkner. And it is one that is of course equally relevant to the Spanish and Italian state monopolies of the period, embodied respectively by RTVE and RAI. But, as we shall see, Italianist scholars' debate on a genre that was so unique as to have initially its own local word (*sceneggiato* preceded the adoption of the Anglicism 'fiction') is somewhat different to that of Hispanists. And I document two major scholars here again, who (like Palacio and Faulkner) are unusual in their defense of Italian television from a discourse of telephobia that remains equally dominant and pervasive in both countries.

In a number of texts and languages Milly Buonanno has treated the classic series or miniseries genre specifically in its national context, even as she insists on the continuing relationship between Italian and foreign (both American and European) television; and David Forgacs' research on Rossellini's historical television dramas goes beyond the definition of genre to examine and incorporate the figure of the auteur, who had in this case, and in spite of his prestigious record in film, explicitly announced that his turn to television was because 'cinema [was] dead'. Based on this friendly attitude to the new medium, Rossellini produced an extensive and neglected body of work in historical fiction for RAI. Forgacs goes into textual detail when analyzing Rossellini's TV work, offering an attention to aesthetics which remains rare in his specialized field but has been proposed elsewhere for general television studies (Jacobs and Peacock 2013).

Such approaches, novel also in Hispanism, allow a new comparative reading of *Fortunata* as a founding example of its genre and as an expression of a film auteur (Mario Camus) who may not have had the international renown of Rossellini but was equally dedicated to both media. They also allow us to make close readings of sequences in a new light for a TV genre often baptized 'cinematic', in something of a back-handed compliment to the electronic medium. Finally I will comment briefly on the legacy of the genre of *sceneggiato* or *serie clásica* for the present day for both Italy and Spain and the question of the classic serial and of *Fortunata* in a new, unforgiving media ecology where literary adaptations are few in number and stand accused of conservative nostalgia.

## The Debate on the *Serie Clásica* in Hispanism: Pedagogy and the Middlebrow

In his pioneering book *Historia de la televisión en España* [A History of Television in Spain], the first to focus on content rather than on institutional questions such as government regulation (2001), Manuel Palacio acknowledges that TV studies in Spain were at the time of writing in their infancy (2001: 13), a condition that was no doubt related to what Palacio coins the 'leyenda negra' [black legend] of 'telebasura' [trash TV] constructed by ideological critics of the medium (2001: 84–85).

Palacio, to the contrary, defends Spanish television's importance as a social history 'from the inside' and as 'individual-collective ritual' (2001: 11). Tracing TV's pre-history, intimately bound up of course with the Dictatorship, Palacio stresses nonetheless that by the 1970s, the very decade of the 'black legend', Spanish television had broadcast series that were created by some thirty film directors, who proved eager to participate in a medium that had recently made the shift from live to taped performance (2001: 87). And, in spite of yet fiercer criticism of RTVE, made possible by increased press freedom, the period between Franco's death and the arrival of the first Socialist government (1975–82) furnished a body of drama that is still firmly anchored in collective memory. *Curro Jiménez*, a historical series on a Robin Hood-style bandit, was a self-proclaimed 'didactic' work on class struggle and anti-imperialism (2001: 88); *La barraca* [The Farmhouse] (1979), a literary adaptation set in the nineteenth century, boasted explicit dialogue on the dangers of civil war that was absent in the source novel itself (2001: 157).

The context of *Fortunata y Jacinta* is thus that of a corpus of big-budget historical series, called 'pedagogical' once more (2001: 153–54) and produced by a monopoly public broadcaster, a corpus that would not survive the commercial competition of private television in the following decade. Palacio defines this pedagogy (which was accredited by literary or historical consultants) as a reworking of the public culture of the present on the basis of the historic 'sedimentation' of the past (2001: 144). The key subgenres here were (as in Italy in an earlier period) exemplary life stories (*Cervantes*, 1981) and literary adaptations (most importantly and lavishly, *Fortunata*) (2001: 153). From Francoism, through the Transition, and into the Socialist era, period drama or in-house 'ficción' was thus the signature feature through which a public service channel and a national TV system sought to lend itself legitimacy after the Dictatorship (2001: 143).

More recently (2012) Palacio has offered the close reading of *Fortunata* (which was, incidentally, a co-production with French public service television) that he did not make in his previous general book and this time in the more precise context of the Transition. More nuanced than contemporary critics of a so-called 'pacto del olvido' [pact of forgetting], Palacio traces in this monumental work the complex relationship between a dynamic political process, a lengthy production history, and a nuanced reception. Thus he describes three stages in the 'grand [TV] narratives' made in the short period of the government of the UCD, the rightist party that took power after the first democratic national elections since the Civil War (1977–81). *Fortunata* is placed in the third stage, described as a 'swerve to the Left', which followed stages heralding 'the return of a liberal Spain' and 'the first approaches to civil conflict' (2012: 306, 313, 317).

In Palacio's account, by 1980, when *Fortunata* was shown, Spain and its state television service were at a turning point: President Adolfo Suárez was facing a constitutional crisis as his young party was falling apart (it would be wiped out at the next general elections); and, lacking a coherent cultural policy from above, RTVE was being taken over by more 'politicized workers' (2012: 318). Leftist positions would now be 'hegemonic', clearly influencing a series that, unlike others at the time, was produced in-house. Although the production team was assisted by the requisite literary consultant, the key figures in the reception of the series were the liberal author Galdós himself (who Palacio claims was by no means unknown during the Dictatorship), screenwriter Ricardo López Aranda, who already had credits in politically progressive film adaptations, and of course director Mario Camus, who specialized in period feature films before and after the Transition (2012: 320). The 'spectacular' production and large budget, more generous per minute than was common even in feature films of the time, combined with a prestige cast to produce a powerful quality effect (2012: 321).

In his public pronouncements to the press Camus was unashamedly political, claiming that the moral of his series was to contrast the 'sterility of the bourgeoisie' with the 'fertility of the people', a portrait of Spain that worked perfectly for both past and present (2012: 321). (In both novel and series the story does indeed climax with the wealthy childless Jacinta taking a new-born infant fathered by her husband from the destitute Fortunata.)

Palacio further cites a 'surprising' scene in the series, this time absent from the source novel. It is of a demonstration in a Madrid street where participants wave a Republican flag and shout '¡Viva la República!' [long live the Republic]. Although this political commentary is framed by a nineteenth-century *mise en scène*, meticulously recreated, it is for Palacio clearly addressed to an immediate present, in which the initial discourse of 'consensus' after the death of Franco was giving way to a Socialist ideology that was encouraged by the 'death rattle' of the rightist UCD (2012: 322). Palacio confirms his reading by citing the rare, positive press notices for the series, including the Socialist *El País* and the Barcelona-based *La Vanguardia*, whose reviewer (his name now Catalanized) was Josep Maria Baget, the same critic who had praised Italian 'sceneggiati' ten years earlier (2012: 324).

Palacio's reading demonstrates how political and production context can change our interpretation of a text that is deceptively familiar (*Fortunata* has remained accessible on VHS, DVD, and now RTVE's website since it was first screened); and, conversely, how the detail of that text can challenge received views of a political period decried by some today as a 'pact of forgetting' and the project of a democratic television held to be 'unfinished business' (Bustamante 2013). Beyond this specific national prism, however, the *serie clásica* or literary adaptation testifies to general questions of cultural distinction and cultural capital that go beyond a particular time and place. This has been the contribution of Sally Faulkner's readings of *Fortunata* which, like Palacio's, have now extended over two decades.

Faulkner's *Literary Adaptations in Spanish Cinema* makes room, in spite of its title, for a lengthy chapter on classic television serials in Spain (2004: 79–125). In general terms she compares film and TV versions of *Fortunata* and contests the naive 'fidelity' criterion, whereby audiovisual versions are valued only for their supposed faithfulness to the literary original (we have already seen that the director and critics of *Fortunata*, anxious for contemporary relevance, were also unconcerned by this criterion). Faulkner also introduces new themes unmentioned by critics like Palacio. One is that of urbanism, especially liminal spaces such as staircases which are sites of encounter for characters of different social classes. Another is gender, with the classic serial a rare point of contact between female protagonists and female audiences (curiously in *Fortunata*, both novel and series, the two titular characters barely meet).

Finally, and anticipating the trend toward aesthetics in TV studies, Faulkner offers a close reading of a single sequence in the novel and adaptation. Focusing once more on an urban space, the scene is when working-class Fortunata, newly married to an impotent invalid, is harassed by her long-term bourgeois lover, the indolent Juanito, even as she is confined in her new home in an unfamiliar area of Madrid (2004: 102–03). Where Galdós imagines transparent walls, facilitating in fantasy the lover's invasion of the apartment, Camus opts for repeated reaction shots of the heroine that reveal her desires and fears.

Faulkner thus combines Palacio's ideological reading, albeit to more general effect, with an aesthetic analysis which respects the specificity of the TV medium without abandoning a comparative approach with its literary support. And in this first book she invokes (2004: 13, 24) Bourdieu's middlebrow (the short cut to cultural distinction) with reference to the scorn voiced by intellectual critics for mass media (only one of whom is cited by Palacio) and the unstable position of Camus's literary adaptations in film and TV (Palacio rather takes for granted Camus' cultural capital even as he acknowledges that the director's work in television has been ignored by Spanish cinema scholars).

Surprisingly, perhaps, Faulkner took this TV-derived analysis and used it as a guiding principle for a *History of Spanish Film* (2013). Subtitled *Cinema and Society 1910–2010*, Faulkner's chronicle places the middlebrow at the center of a film tradition whose specialists are normally focused on the unimpeachable auteurs of high culture, making only rare excursions into popular genres. Most recently she has expanded her analysis to world cinema in an edited collection called *Middlebrow Cinema* (2016). Faulkner's own article in this volume is titled 'Rehearsing for Democracy in Dictatorship Spain: Middlebrow Period Drama 1970–77' (2016: 88–106).

While she concentrates here on film (including a cinematic adaptation of *Fortunata* in 1970 which was co-produced with Italy), Faulkner stresses the connection with television: a newly reconfigured middle-class audience would soon 'shift definitively [from theatrically shown features] to domestic TV viewership' (2016: 88). And her main themes are equally televisual: promoting social justice and reconciliation (2016: 98, 100). Moreover in its role as a 'mirror for today's realities' (a phrase taken from a press review of a Galdós adaptation) Faulkner sees this historical film cycle as 'pedagogical' (97), the term used by Palacio to describe the television of the Transition.

Having sketched the parameters of the scholarly debate (national and transnational) over the *serie clásica* in Spain we can now go on to compare them with those of the *sceneggiato* in Italy, where the ideological and the aesthetic will prove equally contentious.

### The Debate on the *Sceneggiato* in Italian Studies: Indigenization and Auteurism

Milly Buonanno, whom I already cited on quality television in Chapter 3, is the doyenne of Italian TV studies. And like Palacio in Spain she has sought to rescue a huge cultural field from critical neglect and abuse. Her research is at once national (she traces the peculiar development of television in Italy) and transnational (she long headed a comparative research project on European TV drama, the Eurofiction Working Group). Moreover it stretches from the particular and empirical (processes of production and distribution) to the general and theoretical (questions of time and space in television).

In *Italian TV Drama and Beyond* (2012), Buonanno makes a concise claim for the virtues of the *sceneggiato*:

> [...] a crucial component in the 'nation-building' strategy pursued by early Italian television. Be it literary adaptation or period and biographical drama, the *sceneggiato* reenacted for the Italians — a culturally diverse and largely illiterate population in the 1950s — the major historical events and the novelistic tradition in which a once fragmented country turned one nation in relatively recent times was encouraged to recognize the roots — and the routes — of a common history and national belonging. (2012: 7)

The parallels with conditions in Spain, implicitly presented as unique by Hispanist scholars, are clear.

Elsewhere, in an essay called 'The Transatlantic Romance of Television Studies', Buonanno contrasts a long-lasting Italian tradition of quality with its more edgy contemporary US equivalent, now critically dominant. Once more the similarities with Spanish television are clear. It is worth citing at length:

> The tradition of quality in Italian TV drama goes back to the inception of television itself, in the mid 1950s. This means that it has originated and taken root in the historical and cultural humus of public service television, with its ethical commitment to providing a universal service aimed at enhancing public knowledge and education. (2013: 181)

Buonanno goes on to make a special claim for a familiar genre:

> This tradition is premised on the basic conception that quality in TV drama is rooted in an alliance [...] between narrative form and thematic content, which takes shape with the miniseries format [which] incorporates Italian televisual culture's long-lasting and enduring resistance towards seriality [...] the key difference between domestic drama and its American counterpart. The short format of the miniseries [...] therefore holds a distinguished position on the axis of cultural prestige. (2013: 181)

This contrast with the US programming, which would flood Italian schedules in the 1970s, is a crucial one that Hispanist critics have not yet made.

Buonanno is, however, no cultural nationalist. In her first book published in Spanish (*El drama televisivo* [Television Drama]) the main theoretical term is 'indigenization', defined as the way in which audiences actively adopt and adapt foreign (mainly American) content (1999: 41). In her textual analyses she defends the 'multiple realities' of television drama and spectators who, unlike Don Quixote at the puppet show (a favorite Spanish example of Buonanno's (1999: 49)) are perfectly capable of distinguishing between fact and fiction. And in her most theoretically ambitious book, the first to appear in English (*The Age of Television*, 2008), she once more marshals local tactics of reception and transformation against models of cultural imperialism and dependency. Here she invokes 'traveling narratives' as a source of new, if fleeting, senses of place that facilitate 'encounters with the other at differing degrees of proximity' (2008: 102–05). It is a vindication of fluidity and mobility that does not reject the traditional virtues of television: familiarity and proximity. And it focuses on a tradition of quality embodied for some fifty years in the privileged genre of the miniseries, which has both consolidated a national (and continental) TV culture and brought that culture into dialogue with others. Buonanno thus provides a European and transatlantic context for the classic series, which we did not find in Hispanist scholarship.

Buonanno is well aware, of course, that the miniseries is critically allied to film: 'raise[d] to the rank of a cinematographic work' (2013: 181). But it is David Forgacs who has offered a close reading of a case study in the two media which, like Buonanno's research, opens out on to broader questions, in his case auteurism and aesthetics. 'Rossellini's Pictorial Histories' (2011) traces the director's path from his early black-and-white neorealist feature films to his later color television miniseries and asks what the two have in common (2011: 25). At first they seem to display a 'striking switch of style'. The early postwar films (*Paisà* (1946) and *Germany Year Zero* (1948)) show 'spareness, a suspension of dialogue, and [a] concentration on a [real] photographed landscape' (2011: 26). In the later TV dramas (*The Age of the Medici, Blaise Pascal* (both 1972)) to the contrary, even when they show real locations, they are 'dressed up, as in a living museum, with period costumes and details' (2011: 26), even using the optical effect of the mirror shot to combine pro-filmic location with a painted set (2011: 27). Moreover many scenes are 'heavy on dialogue' which Rossellini himself called 'didattici'. While Forgacs comments that in Italian (as in Spanish) the connotation of the word is less 'preachy' than 'didactic' is in English, sequences in which, say, Pascal defends his method of experimental proof are unabashedly educational. This is part of a public service goal also stressed by Buonanno (and Palacio).

Forgacs relates these stylistic differences to Rossellini's 'conversion' to the medium of television. By the 1960s he saw cinema as 'an entertainment Moloch' while TV, 'far from being an instrument of mass distraction, possessed enormous potential as a vehicle for popular teaching' (2011: 29). And in the spite of the apparent discontinuities between Rossellini's early and late work, still Forgacs finds continuities such as a 'sobriety of technical means' (2011: 29). Initially Rossellini the neorealist had avoided beautiful shots for their own sake and held to a 'linear and episodic' narrative style. Subsequently Rossellini the costume dramatist, for economic and aesthetic reasons, still employed long takes and non-professional actors, examples of the supposed 'respect for the real' famously praised by Bazin.

Clunky TV apparently destined for the classroom could thus be (and indeed was) reclaimed by at least one Italian critic as a 'radical form of avant-garde experimentation' (2011: 30). Rossellini, whose *oeuvre* is divided exactly in length between film and television, would not live to see the decline of public service broadcasting and the rise of private networks in the 1980s in Italy (2011: 33), as a little later in Spain, which would soon see his kind of TV confined to a scheduling ghetto throughout Europe.

Forgacs also investigates Rossellini's relationship to developments in the study of history in the period. While the cineaste's period dramas remain attached to great men and their associated Western tradition, they also reveal an interest in collective evolutionary processes (the so-called *longue durée*), in material objects, and in the political use of spectacle (2011: 34). Indeed Forgacs, in what he calls 'the paradox of proximity and distance' (35), claims that while the director's postwar films subjected then recent events to 'ideological reshaping', his later TV works on far-off eras exhibit 'an observational engagement with the ideas and value systems of the past which give them extraordinary power as historical representations' (2011: 36).

Ironically, then, the costume drama (*serie clásica*, *sceneggiato*), so often dismissed as stiff and reactionary, could, like the most ambitious of contemporary feature films (in Forgacs' final words), 'comment on the world and provoke audiences to both emotion and reflection' (2011: 36). We can now, finally, sketch how a Spanish literary adaptation might achieve this ambitious aim suggested by an Italian auteur.

## *Fortunata y Jacinta*: Television Aesthetics and Style

In a characteristic sequence from the first of Mario Camus' ten hour-long episodes of *Fortunata*, Juanito's parents are waiting late at night for their wastrel son to come back to his bourgeois home. Their claustrophobic museum-like drawing room is crammed with furniture and knickknacks, including a curious and no doubt emblematic love seat, which would require its twin occupants to face in opposite directions. There is also a strategically placed mirror on the set which Camus uses to fluidly capture the actors as they move through his carefully crafted *mise en scène*. The fussing mother, played by much-loved veteran Mary Carrillo, rises from her armchair and moves towards the door, followed by the camera, as a family retainer (reflected in the mirror) enters with no news of the erring heir. Following Carrillo once more to the window, there is finally a cut to her point of view: in the street below a carriage pulls up and, to the sound of female laughter, Juanito unsteadily exits.

What is striking about this sequence is that it runs some two minutes without an edit. This leisurely pace attests not only to a public service monopoly broadcasting service, in which creators need not fear viewers be tempted to switch channels to faster fare, but also to a television that clearly aspires to the status of art cinema. As we have seen, the sequence shot was a staple of auteurs such as Rossellini. The lavish decor and costumes, with both exteriors and interiors shot on expansive sets in RTVE's studios at Prado del Rey, also attest to Faulkner's middlebrow virtue of craft and its attendant short cut to cultural capital for aspiring consumers wary of *telebasura*. Viewers who might hesitate to read a novel some thousand pages long can

FIG. 4.1. Ana Belén as Fortunata in Mario Camus' classic serial for
TVE, *Fortunata y Jacinta*

be assured by the abundant and historically attested visuals that they are watching
the best kind of (cinematic) television, worthy of the Galdós whose photograph
appears throughout the series' lengthy opening credits.

What is less clear is Palacio's pedagogic focus or intent in this sequence. Juanito
had been shown uncharacteristically in the very first scene of the series taking part
in a student demonstration which leads to his arrest, an act with abundant echoes
in the tumultuous Transition. But while his parents, anxious to restrain their
son with marriage, are clearly shown as stuffy emblems of the bourgeois sterility
denounced by Camus (an attitude typical of newly hegemonic Leftists), the younger
generation, represented here by a character who proves to be a shiftless idler, is
barely more sympathetic. Impatient spectators will have to wait some hours before
Juanito's encounter (on a staircase) with the fertile, defiant Fortunata. She is played
by Ana Belén, well known to Spanish audiences at the time as a singing star of the
Transition who was an outspoken progressive.

Perhaps Buonanno's 'nation-building' strategy in the *sceneggiato* is helpful
here. Like the Italian audience of the 1950s, Spaniards were (and are) diverse and
fragmented. Juanito and Jacinta's honeymoon trip around the Spanish state, a short
'traveling narrative' which boasts rare authentic locations from Barcelona to Seville,
could be seen as an attempt to craft a public television service for a new nation
and era, even for those viewers outside the capital not partial to the series' minute
recreation of vintage Madrid. Buonanno would also suggest we pay attention here
to the multiple realities of TV fiction (crucially, the coexistence in *Fortunata* of
a recreated conflictive past and a remade democratic present) and to a European

tradition of quality. The latter is signaled explicitly by the international casting of this co-production (Juanito and his father are played by dubbed French actors) and implicitly by an incomplete commitment to seriality, a desideratum Buonanno identifies with American television. Camus' focus (like Galdós') often wanders away from the central characters and locations, with whole episodes neglecting the main plotline to focus on peripheral subplots.

The miniseries thus aspires, as in Italy before Spain, to a special status in the context of a specific, European TV ecology, in an alliance between narrative form and thematic content. And, as in Forgacs' account of Rossellini's 'pictorial histories', *Fortunata* engages closely with both audiovisual technique and historiography. Dialogue-heavy and sparing in action, the series teaches Spanish audiences about their country's convoluted past politics (here engaging in televisual pedagogy), even as its measured pace educates them in deferring immediate gratification, in narrative as in life. While this emphatic slowness imitates glacially evolving historical process (the *longue durée*), the meticulously fashioned *mise en scène* (that curious love seat) attests to material culture and to its associated mentalities as proper objects of history, beyond the chronicles of great men and their grand narratives. Ironically, then, a supposedly cinematic and exceptional television (the *serie clásica*) here circles back to the traditional virtues of 'ordinary' TV: domesticity and everydayness, albeit those of the past. It is a kind of 'observational engagement' that Forgacs saw in Rossellini and a sympathetic critic might find also in the less renowned Camus.

## The Future in the Past

David George recounts how Ana Belén, Camus' Fortunata, addressed an academic conference on Galdós in 2017 (2018: 23). The 'iconic celebrity of the Transition', he writes, insisted on 'the continuing relevance of the author and his novels as a rich source of material for twenty-first century dramas'. But she contrasted the 'quality' programming of the public service past with that of the private present 'echoing the disdain for Spanish television often voiced by intellectuals on the Left' (2018: 23–24). Still identified with the character of Fortunata, Belén reveals how 'the miniseries has come to be inscribed in Spain's popular cultural heritage' (2018: 24). And proof of this are the original daily serials currently playing on Spanish television that are set in the same period, functioning as 'a revised mode of heritage television' and invoking 'collective memories' of the *serie clásica* (2018: 24–25). (One of those serials, mentioned by George, is *El secreto de Puente Viejo*, which, as we saw in Chapter 1, received a loving homage from the telephile Javis in their *Paquita Salas*.)

The classic series in its two variants of great man biography and literary adaptation is now rare indeed on free-to-air television, although in Chapter 3 we saw the first subgenre resurrected somewhat problematically in National Geographic's *Genius: Picasso*. Buonanno cites *La meglio gioventù* [The Best of Youth] (RAI Fiction and Marco Tullio Giordana, 2003) as the last historical series made for Italian television that had ambitions as a national narrative and was 'consecrated' when shown theatrically as a feature film (2013: 181). Yet the example of current

Spanish programming shows us that the period miniseries can mutate into a daily serial which retains some of the formal and ideological characteristics of its more prestigious predecessors from earlier decades.

Moreover research on Italian historical drama, sketched above, reveals that the particular context of the Spanish Transition is not necessary or sufficient to account for the full significance of *Fortunata*. This would clearly benefit from a comparative analysis with other European examples of a genre that is common across the continent, in spite of its varied names, and from a comparative study of auteurs who have made vital contributions, whether willingly or not, to both media. It would be a project parallel to that of Urios-Aparisi and Spani (2020) who focus overwhelmingly on film. But, finally, as Baget suggested so many years ago of the Italian period drama that he recognized even from isolated Francoist Spain as pioneering in a 'new art', film and television, especially in this current age of media convergence, may be not rivals but rather 'friends', as is shown by the unique case of the *sceneggiato/serie clásica*.

## References: Text

BAGET HERMS, JOSÉ MARÍA. 1965. *Televisión, un arte nuevo* (Madrid: Rialp)
BUONANNO, MILLY. 2009. *The Age of Television: Experiences and Theories* (Bristol: Intellect)
———. 2012. *Italian TV Drama and Beyond* (Bristol: Intellect)
———. 2013. 'The Transatlantic Romance in Television Studies and the "Tradition of Quality" in Italian TV Drama', *Journal of Popular Television*, 1.2: 175–89
BUSTAMANTE, ENRIQUE. 2013. *Historia de la radio y la televisión en España: una asignatura pendiente de la democracia* (Barcelona: Gedisa)
FAULKNER, SALLY. 2004. *Literary Adaptations in Spanish Cinema* (London: Tamesis)
———. 2013. *A History of Spanish Film: Cinema and Society, 1910–2010* (London: Bloomsbury)
——— (ed.). 2016. *Middlebrow Cinema* (London: Routledge)
FORGACS, DAVID. 2011. 'Rossellini's Pictorial Histories', *Film Quarterly*, 64.3: 25–36
GEORGE, DAVID R., JR. 2018. 'Fortunata's Long Shadow: The Restoration as Televisual Heritage in *Acacias 38* and *El Secreto de Puente Viejo*', in *Televising Restoration Spain*, ed. by David R. George, Jr. and Wan Sonya Tang (Cham, Switzerland: Palgrave Macmillan), pp. 23–49.
JACOBS, JASON, and STEVEN PEACOCK (eds). 2013. *Television Aesthetics and Style* (New York and London: Bloomsbury)
PALACIO, MANUEL. 2001. *Historia de la televisión en España* (Barcelona: Gedisa)
———. 2012. *La televisión durante la Transición española* (Madrid: Cátedra)
SMITH, PAUL JULIAN. 2006. *Television in Spain: Franco to Almodóvar* (London: Tamesis)
URIOS-APARISI, EDUARDO, and GIOVANNI SPANI (eds). 2020. *Diálogos e influencias: cine y televisión en Italia y en España* (Holden, MA: Quod Manet)

## References: Audiovisual

*Age of the Medici, The.* 1972. Dir. by Roberto Rossellini (RAI Radiotelevisione Italiana)
*barraca, La.* 1979. (RTVE)
*Blaise Pascal.* 1972. Dir. by Roberto Rossellini (RAI Radiotelevisione Italiana)
*Curro Jiménez.* 1976–79. (RTVE)
*Fortunata y Jacinta.* 1980. Dir. by Mario Camus (RTVE/TéléFrance)

*Forsyte Saga, The.* 1967. (BBC)

*Germany Year Zero.* 1948. Dir. by Roberto Rossellini (Tevere Film)

*meglio gioventù, La.* 2003. Dir. by Marco Tullio Giordana (RAI Fiction)

*Paisà.* 1946. Dir. by Roberto Rossellini (OFI)

*vita di Leonardo da Vinci, La.* 1971. Dir. by Roberto Rossellini (RAI Radiotelevisione Italiana)

*secreto de Puente Viejo, El.* 2011–present. (Boomerang/Ida Y Vuelta/Antena 3)

# PART III

# Rewriting Gender on TV and Streaming

# CHAPTER 5

# History Girls:
# Time, Place, and Gender in
# Two Spanish TV Series of 2018

## Two Series, Two Platforms

Two rare female-focused series premiered in Spain near simultaneously in 2018, one (*Arde Madrid* [Madrid is Burning]) from new pay streaming service Movistar+, the other (*La otra mirada* [A Different View]) from heritage free-to-air broadcaster RTVE. I argue in this fifth chapter, the first focusing on gender, that both series conjugate in new and different ways the three themes of historicity, location, and women that are central to Spanish media studies, but are also to more general contemporary cultural studies of that nation.

These three intersecting topics interact with one another and are contradictory in themselves. First, as scholars have documented for Spain, as for other countries, period or costume drama, on television as in film, appeals both to historical authenticity, the testimony to the past, and presentism, a connection with the current circumstance of the viewing public (Lacalle, Castro, and Sánchez 2014). Second, the use of authentic places in such series serves (like their appeal to past periods) as a guarantor of quality and an index of closeness to a national audience, as well as a touristic value for international viewers (Cascajosa Virino 2016). And, finally, 'women's drama' can be defined in at least three different ways: in terms of production, reception, and representation, respectively (Cascajosa Virino and Martínez Pérez 2015). In the period series, then, history can yield to contemporaneity, location to dislocation, and female specificity to a complex negotiation of industry and textuality.

My two fictions also embody different models of distribution and exhibition at a time of radical change and growth in their common televisual medium, a factor which also directly affects their form. The single season of *Arde Madrid* (a second was announced but finally not shot), which is set in the late Francoist era of 1961, consists of just eight episodes running for the half hour familiar from foreign sitcoms. It was filmed wholly on location in the capital and in luminous black and white. *La otra mirada* appeals more conventionally to handsome color costumes and decors of the 1920s that are reconstructed in a Madrid studio, supplemented by picturesque authentic exteriors in Seville. It consisted of a first season of thirteen episodes running for the seventy minutes then still normal for Spanish network television. Following a new trend, its second season's episodes, broadcast in 2019) were reduced to sixty minutes, closer to the internationally standard length for drama and facilitating export to foreign markets. All the episodes have attracted an audience of over one million viewers in their home country.

In this context of a Spanish female-centered narrative that responds more or less explicitly to the #MeToo movement, the new medium of private streaming allowed greater artistic license to the creators of *Arde Madrid* when it came to graphic sexual and verbal content. The period was not unknown on broadcast television (RTVE's long running warhorses *Cuéntame cómo pasó* [Tell Me How it Happened] (2001–) and *Amar en tiempos revueltos* [Love In Difficult Times] (2005–) had both treated the 1960s (Smith 2009)). But the series' premise, of a Hollywood movie star (Ava Gardner) in Francoist Madrid, was unprecedented. It also boasted an unexpected protagonist. After all Gardner, presented here as foul-mouthed and promiscuous, could hardly serve, like the Lorca I studied in Chapter 2, as an exemplary focus for Spanish historical pedagogy.

Conversely *La otra mirada*, a prime-time drama set in a girls' school in Seville made for the public service network that addresses a general audience, could not permit itself such freedom of expression and initially felt familiar to both critics and audiences. Spain's several recent series set in that same decade (the so-called 'happy 1920s'), ably studied by scholars in George and Tang's indispensable collection (2018), included those made by *La otra mirada*'s respected independent production company, Boomerang (we will see in the next chapter that there is another Spanish producer with a track record in costume drama, Bambú).

Yet, if the two series I examine in this chapter align to a large extent with the conventions of their respective and apparently opposite platforms of 'marquee' streaming and 'ordinary' broadcast television (albeit scheduled in prime time, not the afternoon slot to which most costume dramas are confined in Spain), each has hidden connections with the other's genre. Both were made in an era when the literary adaptations of previous decades, the *series clásicas*, had given way to period projects based on original ideas. Moreover, as we shall see, it is the mainstream title that is unapologetically feminist, treating with open didacticism such still controversial topics, at least for its relatively conservative general audience, as rape, abortion, and lesbianism. *La otra mirada*'s educational setting also lends itself naturally to earnest pedagogy, just as *Arde Madrid*'s show business milieu tends towards hedonistic guilty pleasure, for characters and audience alike. Nonetheless both participate in the continuing process of 'working through' social issues that is for British scholar John Ellis (2002) the primary function of the television medium.

### Industrial Analysis: Production and Reception

Before attempting a textual analysis of the two series, let us begin by examining their production and reception, keeping in play the three linked themes of time, place, and gender as we survey the specialist or trade journals and the general press, which remains in Spain a key channel for audience address and public reception. (Like most of the works studied in this book the two series are as yet too recent to have received academic attention.)

*Arde Madrid* was presented and received from the start as a prestige project, attracting attention in three articles in *Variety*, rare coverage for a Spanish series. In 'Movistar+ Expands its International Reach', long-time specialist journalist John Hopewell (the author of a book on post-Francoist cinema back in 1986 called *Out of the Past*) places this single national project within a collective global slate (2018). Claiming that the 'weightiest world premiere' at the San Sebastián Film Festival, the most important in Spain, will be one of the premium pay TV operator's series (*Arde Madrid* is their tenth), Hopewell notes that Movistar+'s parent company is Telefonica, Europe's second biggest telecom.

This 'content drive' has led to 'banner deals' in the US, Europe, and Latin America. The company's director of original fiction (Domingo Corral) says that while his prime aim is to offer clients in Spain 'unique distinctive content', 'international repercussion' is also important for attracting revenues and addressing demand, with Latin American audiences now seeking 'slightly more sophisticated series'. And while the better-known Netflix has just 124 million subscribers worldwide, Movistar, the largest platform in Spain, has 200 million in Latin America alone.

The next month *Variety* returned to the series but this time stressing the gender angle: 'Movistar Plus' Drive into Fiction is Centered on Women'. Hopewell and Emiliano Granada (2018) here write from San Sebastián that the period series set in Madrid's 'little known Dolce Vita' has a 'thoroughly modern feminist filter' that gives it a 'contempo [*sic*] edge and broader attraction'. The creators Paco León and Anna Rodríguez Costa (León is credited as first director, Rodríguez as first screenwriter) say that *Arde Madrid*'s 'heart' is the intimate relation between the free-living and -loving Ava Gardner, resident in the Spanish capital for some fifteen years, and the (fictional) 'Francoist sourpuss' Ana Mari, a member of the Sección Femenina [Female Division] tasked by the regime with spying on the subversive star while posing as her servant.

Rodríguez says that when the couple began to develop the series six years earlier 'priming female characters was rare'. Now, with what she calls 'the new feminist boom', *Arde Madrid* has a 'feminine gaze' (a phrase reminiscent of the title of my second series, *La otra mirada*). Following the 'new strategic direction' of the company, by 2019 40% of Movistar+'s directors, producers, and screenwriters will be women.

Finally *Variety*'s correspondent Granada (2018) interviews the two showrunners in depth in 'Movistar+ Original *Arde Madrid*'s Creators Open Up'. The topic is 'Ava Gardner, Flamenco, and Feminism under Franco'. The journalist says the series 'feels contemporary' but also channels the Spanish film tradition of black neorealist comedy: Luis García Berlanga, Rafael Azcona, and Fernando Fernán Gómez. Rodríguez insists however on her show's new 'feminist discourse' which arises naturally from the characters' development: significantly the male lead (the chauffeur played by León himself) has an 'emotional arc', while female lead Ana Mari's trajectory is more 'active'. And attempting to avoid making a 'public biopic', the creators' focus in their lengthy research was on what they could learn of the intimacy of Gardner's private relationship with her servants. Moreover the company allowed the showrunners 'personal vision and creative freedom', even when it came to shooting in black and white, an unprecedented uncommercial choice, finally greenlighted by Domingo Corral once more.

Interestingly, León, a long time sitcom star here directing his first series, insists even amongst these cinephile references and the associated stress on the 'aesthetic' and 'craft' that he has 'a lot of respect for TV'. Hence the series has a traditional credit sequence, a convention abandoned by most streaming titles. Likewise, if *Arde Madrid* is about 'Spanish identity' (as signaled by its allegiance to a distinctive tradition of Francoist film comedy familiar only to locals) it also connects with international audiences through its perceived 'authenticity'. In this influential trade press coverage, then, time, place, and gender come together to make a prestigious yet potently commercial cocktail via a newly original series for a newly ambitious global telecom company.

The coverage in Spanish specialist website FormulaTV.com offers a more domestic perspective, detailing the vicissitudes of the production process. In a report from an event hosted by ALMA, the Spanish screenwriters' union, Rodríguez is cited as saying that the project had first been offered to Mediaset, parent company of broadcast network Telecinco, with whom her partner León had a long association as actor in massively popular sitcom *Aída* (Telecinco, 2005–14) and as director in two low-budget feature films (*Carmina o revienta* [Carmina or Blow Up] (2012) and *Carmina y amén* [Carmina II] (2014)), also shot in black and white, plus a more conventional color comedy (*Kiki, el amor se hace* [Kiki, Love to Love] (2016)).

When, as was expected, the mainstream broadcaster passed on this envelope-pushing project, the pair pitched *Arde Madrid* to Netflix, which considered their show 'too expensive' for what would have been the streaming giant's Spanish premiere. It was only then that the more supportive Movistar+ stepped in (Alabadí 2018). Confirming its special status, *Arde Madrid* would prove to be the first of the telecom's series to be premiered simultaneously in Spain and in ten Latin American territories (FormulaTV 2018a).

Much of FormulaTV's coverage focuses on casting. The site sketches for Spaniards the career credits of Debi Mazar, the American indie film and cable TV star who plays Ava Gardner and notes that the cameo role of the Duchess of Alba (a decades-long staple of Spain's gossip magazines) will be piquantly played in the series by her own daughter (FormulaTV 2018b). More importantly, perhaps, and directly challenging the division between 'marquee' streaming content and 'ordinary TV', is the fact that no fewer than four of the former cast of *Aída*, León's massively popular sitcom for Telecinco (including the much-loved Carmen Machi, the title character), will appear at some point in his premium series, a reunion that Spanish audiences are highly likely to recognize and appreciate (FormulaTV 2018d). Likewise, linking period show and contemporary culture, the site reveals that singer Rosalía, baptized 'the artist of the moment', will contribute her version of a traditional flamenco number to one episode (Arenas 2018).

FormulaTV.com also documents the publicity process for this streaming series, extending its niche reach into traditional mainstream and social media. On one broadcast talk show Mazar had recounted a 'scatological' anecdote worthy of her raunchy version of Gardner in the series. And León had 'stripped bare' his cast on Instagram, challenging them to pose nude with him for the platform (Bertol 2018).

Finally, the site's specialist review, intended for TV professionals and devoted fans, focuses on the series' deft visualization of its premise: in one emblematic sequence a shot of a portrait of Francisco Franco shifts with racking focus to a rudimentary dildo held in the hand of dowdy maid Ana Mari (Rodera 2018), played by an Inma Cuesta who is unrecognizable here after her sensual role in *La novia*. The theme of the miniseries is thus the contrast between Francoist repression and the tantalizing sexual liberation that, in a cliché of the period, is said to 'invade' a still dour and moralizing Spain.

Crucially, however, the reviewer writes that even from their fully modern perspective the twin showrunners treat their period characters without condescension, depicting the banality of everyday life at a time of poverty, illiteracy, and deprivation without resorting to parody. Moreover León advocates sexual liberation also at the present time when, or so he claims to the journalist, Spaniards are hesitating as to whether to revert to self-censorship. Even this highly crafted period piece, then, apparently a depiction of a long lost and alien Spain, is thought to have a strong element of presentist commentary.

It is instructive to compare these specialist accounts with the generalist coverage by daily newspaper of record *El País*, once hostile to the television medium but now anxious to connect with series-loving younger readers. Several of the articles are by Elsa Fernández Santos, a former film critic who, in a sign of the times, has been reassigned to the TV beat.

In a heavily illustrated report for the daily's Sunday magazine, Fernández Santos (2017) declares the strength of the link between series and audiences to be 'a mystery' and appeals to *Variety* to justify the 'Renaissance of Spanish television' via the 'fiction strategy' of Movistar+. *El País*'s continuing resistance to taking local television seriously in its own terms is shown by the article's title which cites cult series 'made in Spain', giving that phrase in English. Yet the showrunners are cited as saying that they 'want to talk about Spain, about what it was and what we are'. And the León who claims elsewhere to 'have a lot of respect for TV' is quoted in this still telephobic context as saying 'another type of television is possible'.

*El País*'s focus is fully on León, long a star of broadcast TV and social media, to the detriment of his less visible female partner, who features equally in the trade press. One piece accompanies the director-actor on a tour of Madrid locations, whether well-known bars and *tablaos flamencos* such as Chicote and Villa Rosa or luxury shops such as Loewe in the Gran Vía (Pastor 2018). In another interview León invokes his hardscrabble childhood in Seville as 'street' background for his working-class chauffeur character, branded a 'chulo' [pimp] in the series (Ruiz Mantilla 2018). A further breathless profile, charting twenty-four hours in the life of Anna Castillo (who plays Gardner's young pregnant maid) stresses presentism once more: she is named 'the actress of the moment' (Cuesta Torrado 2019). Such fashion spreads (Castillo takes time out between receiving awards to pose in designer finery) are clearly aimed at connecting with the female audience who will be targeted by the series.

Finally, a lengthy piece on the series' seductive art design inadvertently calls attention to a hidden conflict between historical authenticity and narrative functionality. It seems that Gardner's shiny modernist apartment in the show, a glass and chrome shrine to her disruptive presence in a traditionalist Spain, could not be further from the 'classical' Madrid home the historical figure kept in real life (Bargueño 2019).

*La otra mirada* was much less of a media event than *Arde Madrid*, lacking as it did a film festival premiere at home and press praise abroad. Yet it also leans heavily on the costume of costume drama and on the visual pleasure of its carefully crafted settings. Indeed at RTVE's press conference announcing the series, the cast, unusually, came garbed in their handsome period wardrobe. FormulaTV's report (2018e) followed the broadcaster's executives in stressing the 'important female content' of the series (most unusually all four protagonists are women) and its presentism, enabling viewers to 'think about what it means to be a woman' and to 'compare the situation in another period with the present day'. And, in an inadvertent parallel with *Arde Madrid*, the premise is of a modern woman (the well-travelled, trouser-wearing Teresa) whose arrival disrupts a traditionalist setting (in this case the provincial girls' academy). Likewise the progressive Manuela has just taken over as principal from her conservative mother and will see her authority challenged in an 'election' by her old-school colleague Luisa (Spanish women's failure to achieve suffrage is one of the political issues repeatedly referenced in the opening episodes).

The central school set is convincingly recreated in a Madrid studio. But the report calls attention once more to the authentic historic and touristic locations in Seville on frequent display in the series, which will serve both as recognizable references to locals and a competitive advantage for the international TV market: the gardens of the Reales Alcázares [Royal Palaces], the Puente de Triana [Triana Bridge], and the Plaza de España (shown in a digital effect as still under construction).

One interesting structural point in the scripting, not so evident to viewers as the picturesque visuals, is related to the large cast that is required to fill the series' lengthy running time: each of the co-equal adult protagonists is allotted three starring episodes in the season (the finale features all four). And in its review of the pilot (Alcaraz 2018) FormulaTV mentioned the 'mystery' element in the plotting (the first episode begins with the murder of the Spanish ambassador in Lisbon) and called attention to producer Boomerang's long track record in successful period fiction, such as the lavish female-led miniseries *El tiempo entre costuras* [The Time In Between] (Antena 3, 2013–14) (see Smith 2016). In the site's subsequent survey of social media response to the pilot (FormulaTV 2018c) viewers enthusiastically praise *La otra mirada*'s 'female protagonists and full-on feminism'. This fierce fan commitment came in spite of the fact that the pilot premiered to a relatively 'modest' share of 9.6% and rating of 1,620,000 (Movistar+, which like its rival Netflix relies on subscription income, rarely releases audience figures).

Coverage in *El País* stressed not the production company (Boomerang) but the heritage distributor (RTVE), insistently repeating a word ('feminism') that no longer seems to frighten producers or audiences and is no longer qualified by appeals to universalism. The paper's report on the press conference (Peiró 2018) cited 'period feminism' and complained only that too few women were hired as writers and directors for the series (it was a criticism addressed by the arrival of an all-female writing room in the second season). The newspaper's interviews with the actors invoked 'feminist lessons from the 1920s' (Marcos 2018) and its review 'the women that RTVE needs' (Ruiz de Elvira 2018). This last piece states bluntly that a 'feminist series' is 'necessary' in prime time and on public television. And it calls attention to 'changing times' in Spanish streaming series (including Movistar+) that require the state broadcaster to make changes too.

This transformation includes an increasingly 'international' projection of titles, a potential later confirmed by the positive coverage of the series' 'feminist perspective' in markets such as Argentina (Parati 2019). RTVE, then, hitherto notoriously conservative, is thus starting to be read within and to react to the private services whose projects are more readily granted prestige than those of the still despised 'ordinary' public broadcaster. And an essential part of public service is now taken to be an outspoken feminism.

Yet our two exemplary titles have much in common, reflecting as they do a newly political consensus around time, place, and female-focused fiction, even in the once conservative genre of costume drama. And there is a hidden connection in the casting between the two series. Anna Castillo (*Arde Madrid*'s younger of the two maids) and Macarena García (*La otra mirada*'s equally youthful principal) are known for their joint participation in works for theatre, film, and television directed by García's brother Javier Ambrossi and her brother-in-law Javier Calvo, the celebrity pair universally known in Spain as 'los Javis' whom I examined in my first chapter. Sharing the frame in *Paquita Salas*, the Javis' groundbreaking mockumentary for Netflix, the two actors ('artists of the moment') provide a bridge between mainstream heritage and niche innovation for producers and consumers alike. The link would be made explicit when the Javis, a very contemporary real-life gay couple, made an unlikely cameo as film directors, partners in work as in life, in a second season episode of *La otra mirada*.

Fig. 5.1. Ava Gardner's three servants in Movistar+'s miniseries *Arde Madrid*. From left: Ana Mari (Inma Cuesta), Pilar (Anna Castillo), and Manolo (showrunner Paco León)

## Dark Comedy: *Arde Madrid*

Streaming series are exempted from the strict demands of broadcast television with regard to the length of seasons and episodes. Yet *Arde Madrid*, relatively faithful like its co-creator León to traditional TV, keeps to a US standard length of thirty minutes' duration for each of the short-form episodes that dropped on 8 November 2018. And, as FormulaTV's critic mentions (Rodera 2018), its development is episodic, with each installment posing and resolving a central plot point or enigma and with continuing plotlines lightly sketched.

Thus the first episode (whose title 'Poco católica' [Not So Well] puns on the irreligious American star's inappropriate behavior in Spain) sets up the odd couple of plain, lame maid Ana Mari and louche, sexy chauffeur Manolo as undercover spies who present themselves as a married couple to work as servants in Ava Gardner's lavish home.

And it puts into play what will prove to be a long-running McGuffin of Manolo's attempt to smuggle an illicit consignment of American whiskey bankrolled by a criminal Roma family. Citing an item of traditional Spanish gastronomy little known to foreign viewers, Episode 2 ('I love mojama' [I Love Dried Tuna]) develops the 'deep' plotline of the whiskey, linking it to Gardner, when the Roma boss asks the indebted Manolo for a pair of the star's (soiled) panties. Meanwhile young maid Pilar is revealed to be pregnant via a picturesque and archaic test involving ovulating frogs.

Episode 3 ('Puta paya' [Non-Gypsy Slut], a reference to the supposedly immoral, non-gypsy American) sees the servants invited to the First Communion of the

Roma's daughter, where they learn that his wife sees the panties as evidence of her husband's affair with Gardner. She has asked in recompense for a valuable necklace the star has worn on a magazine cover. Episode 4, 'Directo fiesta' [Live from the Party], which boasts one of several tour de force festive scenes, has Eva attend the raucous baptism of the child of local star Lola Flores, in the course of which the star loses her necklace in the car chauffeured by Manolo. We have now reached the midpoint of the series.

In Episode 5 (the self-explanatory 'Muy americana' [A Very American Woman]) Manolo commissions a copy of the necklace and Pilar is taken to see a nun who has arranged for her future child to be adopted by a respectable married couple (inexplicably, one of the prospective parents is played by a man in drag, a casting choice anticipated by and reminiscent of the Javis' *Paquita Salas*). In Episode 6 'Más flores que la Virgen' [More Flowers than the Virgin] a much feted and very bored Ava arrives to judge a beauty contest in Mallorca, while, left alone in Madrid, Ana Mari and Manolo become more intimate.

In Episode 7 ('Dios es dios y yo soy yo' [God is God and I Am Me]) Ava returns from her trip and Manolo delivers the two necklaces, original and fake, to the star and the Roma. Gardner also arranges a discreet (and unseen) abortion for Pilar and attends an event in Madrid where she publicly signs a contract for real-life movie *55 Days at Peking* (Nicholas Ray, 1953). Its title comically attracts the attention of the clueless anti-Communist Francoists, unaware that the film is set not in the current Maoist era but in the days of the Boxer Rebellion.

Finally in 'What's autorización?' [What's 'Permission'?] Gardner hosts an epic party, complete with celebrities, Romas, and bemused goat, ostensibly in memory of Hemingway but without the official permission required for such an event at the time. Left to brood over the empties in the early hours, gruff Manolo proposes marriage to downtrodden Ana Mari, who firmly rejects him. Now she wishes only to live her own life to the full.

From the evidence of this synopsis, then, it is striking that the Gardner character has no deep plotline of her own beyond the hardly compelling question of whether she will sign up for the new movie. And important here is the focalization to which the screenwriters are consistent throughout: we see and learn of Ava only from the perspective of the servants (especially Ana Mari), who emerge as the true protagonists of the series. Narrative tension is consistently deflated (Pilar's abortion, the termination of the pregnancy that she had long feared, has no negative consequences). And the series' episodic structure mimics both the hallowed Spanish literary tradition of the picaresque (Manolo is, like León's character in *Aída*, a classic trickster) and the dark comedies of Berlanga and Fernán Gómez (also shot in black and white) with their ensemble casts, crowded group shots, and casually developed plots.

As in Spanish neo-realism, then, the narrative is developed as much in visual as in plot terms. The rack focus between the Franco portrait and the primitive dildo signals without the need for dialogue Ana Mari's growing sexual awakening in spite of the pressure of a still repressive regime, while the contrast between Eva's modern furnishings and the traditional home of Juan Perón below (the star and the exiled President were real-life neighbors) exemplifies the contrast between American freedoms and Latin dictatorships, whatever the continent.

These divisions are progressively blurred, however. Eva is variably skilled in Spanish (aware of the specialized idiomatic meaning of 'no estar católico' [not feeling so well] at one point, unable to string together a simple sentence at others). And the poster for the series shows her with chocolate from a phallic *porra* [large churro] dripping from her lips (the modest Spanish housekeepers cower behind), another culinary reference foreign audiences are unlikely to recognize. The American star's enthusiasm for Spanish gastronomy (and music) testifies to a cross-cultural traffic that also leaves its trace in circular plot points that transcend the modest McGuffin of the whiskey-panties-necklace.

For example, at the moving final moment of one episode a drink-sodden Ava makes a bilingual speech to her skeptical servant defending women's rights to personal freedom and sexual pleasure. It is dialogue that foreshadows Ana Mari's rejection of a marriage proposal from the man who has aided her sexual awakening but will never allow her the liberty to which she newly aspires. As the showrunner herself noted, the man's arc here is emotional (the brutish Manolo shows signs of sensitivity), the woman's active (the timid Ana Mari will strike out bravely on her own). The finale is also defiantly open: we are shown neither the new life of Ana Mari, single but unafraid in Madrid, nor that of Ava in the London which she speaks of moving to in the series, as she would in real life.

The plot is loosely structured, beyond conventional causal progression, by thematic articulation. Historical references are restricted to everyday life (the bizarre frog test) or to show business (Lola Flores' baptism party). And period setting is of course attested to by the conspicuous craft of the *mise en scène*, which is accurate to the time if not to the actual circumstances of the star's residence. The only reference to events in political history is one directly relevant to the series' premise: Ana Mari's superior at the Sección Femenina (played by a smirking Carmen Machi) notes with mixed satisfaction and suspicion that 'The Americans are our friends now'. As is well known to historians (but not perhaps to modern Spanish audiences), after isolating post-War Spain as a Fascist fellow traveler, the USA would in the 1960s accept it as an anti-Communist ally.

Typically the plot condenses into its dramatic action the key themes of time, place, and gender. In the very first sequence Ana Mari (still at the Francoist Sección Femenina) is seen lecturing her young charges on the normality of male violence: if her husband beats her, his wife should ask herself what she has done to deserve it. Access to abortion and contraception is shown to be available only to wealthy foreigners and their protégées. Verbal abuse of women and the disabled is ubiquitous, with Ana Mari constantly insulted as 'coja' [lame].

Class conflict is shown silently but resonantly in the contrast in the *mise en scène* between the greasy *churrerías* [churro stalls] of the servants and the glamorous nightclubs of their masters. The surprisingly prominent Roma theme is important here. The series suggests the existence of a vibrant artistic subculture, at once admired and despised, parallel to and connected with that of the milieu of showbiz folk, who are both worshipped and scorned by the joyless Francoist establishment.

Finally, then, *Arde Madrid* does not benefit only from its streaming service's expressive liberties (constant foul language in English and Spanish, male frontal nudity). It also exploits the same creative freedoms (black-and-white photography, episodic narrative) that Paco León had also explored in his pair of low-budget feature films in order to make a darkly humorous televisual comment on women's oppression by and resistance to the Francoist regime.

## Enlightened Drama: *La otra mirada*

The thirteen seventy-minute episodes of the first season of *La otra mirada*, screened in Spanish prime time at 10.40 pm on Wednesdays from 25 April 2018, required of their broadcast viewers a much greater investment of time than did *Arde Madrid* of its subscribers, who could choose to binge the eight short-form episodes whenever they wished. RTVE's series was, moreover, integrated into a still familiar domestic timescape in which weekly mass viewers were held captive by Spanish networks until midnight.

This regularity and domesticity of consumption presupposes a lengthy incorporation of the series into the everyday life of fans over some three months, a factor that promotes intense identification with the characters and their interlinked plotlines. While its audience was relatively modest for free-to-air television (although much greater than that for niche streaming), *La otra mirada* retained, as mentioned earlier, a rating over one million viewers throughout and the finale took a share of 9.9%, higher than the pilot. The arc of this first season thus secured the fidelity of its fans, the key aim for broadcast series fiction.

Where *Arde Madrid* employs the McGuffin of the whiskey consignment and necklace to lend a semblance of continuity to an episodic structure based more on visuals and psychology than on narrative dynamics, *La otra mirada* employs a mystery device to unify its lengthy arc, handing out new plot points in flashback as the series advances and resolving the plotline only in the last minutes of the final episode. Thus we learn, gradually, that an ambassador murdered in the opening sequence is new teacher Teresa's father and that a scrap of paper she discovered in his hand is the reason for her arrival at the Academy. This mystery structure is reminiscent of a previous successful Spanish period series, *Gran Hotel* [Grand Hotel] (Bambú/Antena 3, 2011–13), in which the brother of a victim sought to investigate her murder, also by going undercover.

Strikingly, however, and revealing its distance from the gender conservativism inherited from telenovela, *La otra mirada* does not contain the traditionally taboo cross-class romance still featured by *Gran Hotel*: the teachers and pupils of the wealthy academy restrict their often conflictive and inappropriate partners to their own social sphere. Teresa's ongoing affair with the school's handsome handyman provokes no dramatic tension and is a sign only of her liberated sexuality. The first episode is named for her transgressive modern tastes: 'Tabaco, pantalones, y jazz' [Tobacco, Trousers, and Jazz].

Fig. 5.2. The four teachers of TVE's period drama *La otra mirada*. From left: Luisa
(Ana Wagener), Manuela (Macarena García), Teresa (Patricia López Arnaiz), and
Ángela (Cecilia Freire)

As in *Arde Madrid*, then, and in spite of the intermittent mystery strand, the
focus is driven more by psychology than strict causality. Each of the four adult
protagonists is presented with dilemmas that require their characters to develop.

Globetrotting Teresa (Patricia López Arnaiz), who has always resisted personal
commitment in spite of her fierce political activism, will remain in Seville after she
comes to care deeply for her colleagues and her charges at the all-female academy.
Veteran Luisa (Ana Wagener), a widow abused by her wastrel son, will come to
question her conservative attitudes to work and family. Manuela (Macarena García),
the new principal, struggles to modernize the school and break free from the
apparently kindly husband who sees her only as the future mother of children she
herself does not want (she is driven to use a primitive contraceptive that wrecks
her health). Finally, most movingly and dramatically, Ángela (Cecilia Freire), an
apparently happily married wife and mother of five, will have a transformatory
affair with a female painter.

*La otra mirada* thus points optimistically to the possibilities of social change in
the period, with its Academy even visited by María de Maeztu, real-life pioneer of
women's education and defender of divorce. But the series insists nonetheless on the
uncompromising historical limits to women's freedom: there can be no place for the
lesbian couple in the Seville of 1920. And a traumatic Easter-set episode (the ninth),
in which Ángela's forbidden affair is revealed and she suffers separations from her
lover, husband, and children, is appropriately titled 'Viacrucis' [Way of the Cross].

The six pupils also, played by previously unknown actors, are given plotlines
that combine psychological development with political issues yet more dramatic

than those of their teachers. One is forced to abandon the boy she loves to marry her parents' choice of partner; another shyly romances an unseen suitor through the small ads of a contacts magazine (he will prove to be Luisa's brutish son); and, in the longest running and most dramatic plotline, a third will suffer and report a rape by the son of one of Seville's most respected families.

Acknowledging once more the historical constraints of such plotlines (can the school afford to support its abused pupil, alienate its paying parents, and challenge the entrenched powers that be in court?), the series also takes care to connect its scripts with contemporary controversies. The perilous contact magazine is a clear counterpart of internet dating and the rape victim is shamed by the distribution of revealing drunken photos by her abuser in an evident precedent of web-posted 'revenge porn' (the modern-sounding title of this fourth episode is 'El derecho a la intimidad' [The Right to Privacy]).

Most prominently the series' rape plotline echoes point by point a long-running real-life case that convulsed Spain in 2018, the same year that *La otra mirada* aired, and which provoked massive street protests by women: the gang rape of a young woman by a group calling themselves 'La Manada' [the Wolf Pack]. The young victim in the series is smeared for her revealing dress and alcohol use, condemned for her failure to resist her abuser, and, finally, affronted by the lenient penalty the man receives (in 2019 La Manada's sentence would be reviewed and lengthened) (Rincón 2019). The trial episode, a little more than half way through the season (Episode 8: 'La primera y última palabra' [The First and Last Word]), is *La otra mirada*'s dramatic highlight.

These highly charged gender issues are intertwined once more with time and place. Viewers were no doubt as shocked as the female characters to learn that a male teacher, then something of a rarity, should, by law, be paid twice their salary. And the primitive birth control of the time threatens women's health. Unable to vote in national elections, the Academy is reduced to electing their new principal from two candidates. The conservative location of Seville is vital here, far as it is from María de Maeztu's pioneering Residencia de Señoritas [Young Ladies Hall of Residence] in progressive Madrid, the lesser-known female equivalent of the Residencia de Estudiantes attended by Lorca, Buñuel, and Dalí mentioned in my second chapter. It is at a louche party where flamenco performers entertain idle *señoritos* [rich kids] that the schoolgirl is intoxicated and violated. Characters walk through the exquisite gardens of the Generalife or sip local *fino* [dry sherry] in the geranium-decorated streets of Santa Cruz, both key tourist attractions, discussing all the while their urgent personal and professional problems.

In one moving fantasy sequence the lesbian lovers, who must of course hide from the crowd, stage a romantic dance in the very public setting of a quay of the Guadalquivir in the center of Seville. Problematically, then, these authentic locations come with a historical charge that is at once intensely pleasurable and deeply oppressive. Typically the series in its Easter episode shows respect for the tradition of the *pasos* or processional floats (the sympathetic caretaker is a member of a *cofradía* [brotherhood]) even as it, somewhat blasphemously, proposes the lesbian mother as a new sacrificial victim: re-enacting the Stations of the Cross, Ángela will fall to her knees in a church nave as her children are led away.

The costumes of costume drama are here more visible than ever. Loosely inspired by Mariano Fortuny and Paul Poiret, the reforming designers of women's dress after the First World War, the series' clothes drape women's bodies in loosely flowing and richly colored velvets and chiffon. Such exquisite wardrobe might seem implausible in the context: surely not all provincial teachers could be so fashion-conscious? And were glamorous social occasions requiring elaborate formal dress ('the Autumn Dance', 'the Masked Ball') quite so frequent? Yet, far from being a distraction from the series' social issues, this *mise en scène* could be read as furthering those aims: beyond the discrete topics of rape, divorce, labor rights, and contraception, the general moral of *La otra mirada* is women's right to sensual pleasure (we are shown an early sex education class which focuses on the female orgasm).

Enticing viewers with an exquisite production design for which it sees no need to apologize, the series also encourages them to reflect on the possible gap between the aesthetic and the political, on the damage done by defining and confining women as objects, not subjects, of desire. The twelfth episode ('Ser mujer' [Being a Woman]) is the most explicit here: when the girls take to painting their faces like the models they have seen in Parisian magazines, principal Manuela tells them that lipstick is not wrong, but should be worn to give pleasure to the wearer not to the male onlooker. Likewise Ángela only recognizes her true lesbian self when she is painted Fauve-style by her future lover. And the frequent classes devoted to fine arts in the series (of painting appreciation, of amateur drama, and, later, of film analysis) are the equivalents of the showy showbiz scenes of *Arde Madrid*, which also have social implications beyond their transparent visual pleasure.

As taught by the trouser-wearing Teresa, these art history classes facilitate a reflexive meditation on the political implications of artistic process for characters and audience alike. It is a self-conscious process heavily signaled by *La otra mirada*'s credit sequence, which shows paintbrushes sketching women's eyes in artistic styles from realist to Cubist, quite literally depicting a diversity of 'other looks'.

### Three Themes

Milly Buonanno, the most respected scholar of European television, whom we have already cited in Chapter 4, has defended period fiction from its many detractors, arguing that TV is a 'time machine' that offers viewers access to 'multiple realities' that 'organize experience into a narrative form' (1998: 119–21, 70–72). This is clearly confirmed by my two series. A recent history of feminism in Spain claims that only 2% of the population considers themselves feminist, although its reviewer notes that some respondents may feel more uncomfortable with the term than they do with a progressive gender agenda (Everly 2019: 398). It is thus remarkable that television, especially free-to-air public television, should now be so overtly feminist, even to the extent of embracing without apology the word itself as we saw in the press coverage of both series.

The second season of *La otra mirada*, which focused on abortion, went even further than the first. Officially promoted hashtags for individual episodes which began with a handy acronym for the series' title included '#LOMaborto' [#LOMabortion] and (coinciding with LGBT+ Pride week) '#LOMorgullo' [#LOMpride]. RTVE, long dismissed as 'casposo' [antiquated] (a word used of the public service broadcaster in *El País*'s otherwise positive review of the series [Ruiz de Elvira] (2018)), entered bravely into the fray of current political controversies after a national election which had seen the emergence for the first time of an extreme right party in Spain, Vox. This trend is in line with RTVE's lengthy history of pedagogy in progressive politics that the founding historian of Spanish television, Manuel Palacio, has traced back to the Transition to democracy, as we also saw in Chapter 4 (2001, 2012).

Women protagonists and period series have long been a special focus of drama programming in Spain, much more so than in other Spanish-speaking countries. And we will see in the next chapter that this trend extends unbroken onto the global platform of Netflix as a competitive advantage for the nation. Moreover both themes have been the central subject of successive years of annual reports on the field made by international research group OBITEL, the Observatorio Iberoamericano de Ficción Televisiva [Iberoamerican Survey of Television Drama], one of which cites 'The Boom of Fiction Set in the Past' (OBITEL 2015; Lacalle, Castro, and Sánchez 2014). And the question of feminism or post-feminism in costume drama, especially in biopic, has, as we saw in Chapter 3, been much treated by scholars of film and television in other territories, most especially the UK (Polaschek 2013).

Yet the intensity of this tendency is clearly greater in the two Spanish series studied here than elsewhere. Meanwhile Spanish TV fiction, which once took place in generic unmarked locations dismissed by critics as 'planeta series' [series planet], has now embraced specific geographical places within the Peninsula (Cascajosa Virino 2016), as is clearly the case in the richly detailed visions of Madrid and Seville here. In my two examples, though it is not the first time that time, place, and gender are explored in Spanish television, they are clearly presented in new and challenging ways that track a changing national media ecology.

Most important is that these three themes establish a connection between the new streaming platforms, whose high-profile 'marquee' projects are a focus of journalists and academics alike, and traditional broadcast networks, whose 'ordinary' titles are often overlooked in spite of their continued massive audiences and integration into the rhythm of national everyday life. While *La otra mirada*'s youthful idealism and tragic romance could hardly be further from the worldly, sarcastic tone of *Arde Madrid*, both series offer new and startling accounts of periods in twentieth-century Spanish history (a 1920s that was not so happy for working women, a 1960s that offered a chance at least of female empowerment).

Moreover both dramas offer high production values and spectacular visual pleasure, though once more of very different kinds, from lushly decorative color to starkly modern monochrome. They prove not only that, technically, Spanish television has no reason to envy cinema, but that the aesthetic can sometimes be integrated into the social, not distracting from but rather reinforcing its political effect. Even as they offer sophisticated and stylish entertainment, then, Spanish television's history girls of 2018 engage in a continuing and parallel process of working through the key contemporary issues that concern current female publics, a process that no other audiovisual medium can rival. We can now go on to see how Spain's established strengths in a television drama made on and for women enabled the country to compete with such success in the unforgiving global arena created by Netflix.

## References: Text

ALABADÍ, HÉCTOR. 2018. 'Arde Madrid se presentó inicialmente a Mediaset', FormulaTV, 26 October <https://www.formulatv.com/noticias/arde-madrid-presento-inicialmente-mediaset-evitar-enfado-paolo-vasile-85280/> [accessed 21 February 2021]

ALCARAZ, MARIPAZ. 2018. 'Crítica de La otra mirada', FormulaTV, 25 April <https://www.formulatv.com/noticias/79163/critica-la-otra-mirada-exito-epoca-tintes-misterio/> [accessed 21 February 2021]

ARENAS, ÓSCAR. 2018. 'Rosalía ha versionado a un clásico del flamenco para la serie de Paco León', FormulaTV, 7 November <https://www.formulatv.com/noticias/rosalia-versiona-cancion-flamenco-arde-madrid-85694/> [accessed 21 February 2021]

BARGUEÑO, MIGUEL ÁNGEL. 2019. 'La casa de Ava Gardner que burló la represión del franquismo', El País, 28 January <https://elpais.com/elpais/2019/01/24/icon_design/1548353205_125181.html> [accessed 21 February 2021]

BERTOL, NOELIA. 2018. 'Paco León desnuda al elenco de Arde Madrid', FormulaTV, 6 November <https://www.formulatv.com/noticias/paco-leon-desnuda-elenco-seguidores-arde-madrid-instagram-85651/> [accessed 21 February 2021]

BUONANNO, MILLY. 1998. The Age of Television: Experiences and Theories (London: Intellect)

CASCAJOSA VIRINO, CONCEPCIÓN. 2016. 'Series españolas: signos de renacimiento', Caimán, March, pp. 22, 24

—— and NATALIA MARTÍNEZ PÉREZ (eds). 2015. Mujeres en el aire: haciendo televisión (Madrid: Tecmerin)

FERNÁNDEZ SANTOS, ELSA. 2017. 'Se buscan creadores para series de culto "made in Spain"', El País Semanal, 3 December <https://elpais.com/elpais/2017/11/24/eps/1511550767_373726.html> [accessed 21 February 2021]

EVERLY, KATHRYN. 2019. REVIEW OF SILVIA BERMÚDEZ and ROBERTA JOHNSON (eds), A New History of Iberian Feminism, Revista de Estudios Hispánicos, 53.1: 397–99

FORMULATV. 2018A. 'Arde Madrid será la primera series de Movistar+ con estreno simultáneo en España y Latinoamérica', FormulaTV, 30 October <https://www.formulatv.com/noticias/arde-madrid-primera-serie-movistar-estreno-simultaneo-latinoamerica-85432/> [accessed 21 February 2021]

——. 2018B. 'Eugenio Martínez de Irujo interpretará a su madre', FormulaTV, 12 March <https://www.formulatv.com/noticias/77740/eugenia-martinez-irujo-interpretara-madre-duquesa-alba-arde-madrid/> [accessed 21 February 2021]

——. 2018C. 'Gran acogida de La otra mirada: mujeres como protagonistas y feminismo a tope. Muy bien, TVE', FormulaTV, 26 April <https://www.formulatv.com/noticias/79210/gran-acogida-la-otra-mirada-mujeres-protagonistas-feminismo-tope-bien-tve/> [accessed 21 February 2021]

——. 2018D. 'Miren Ibarguren, Carmen Machi, Paco León y Eduardo Casanova se reúnen tras Aída', FormulaTV, 3 August <https://www.formulatv.com/noticias/82597/arde-madrid-reunion-aida-movistar-paco-leon-carmen-machi-eduardo-casanova/> [accessed 21 February 2021]

——. 2018E. 'RTVE presenta *La otra mirada*, una serie de época con un gran contenido femenino muy importante', *FormulaTV*, 6 March <https://www.formulatv. com/noticias/77546/rtve-presenta-la-otra-mirada-serie-epoca-componente-femenino-importante/> [accessed 21 February 2021]

CUESTA TORRADO, SARA. 2019. '24 horas con Anna Castillo, la actriz del momento', *El País Semanal*, 16 February <https://elpais.com/elpais/2019/02/08/eps/1549651910_094278. html> [accessed 21 February 2021]

ELLIS, JOHN. 2002. *Seeing Things: Television in the Age of Uncertainty* (London: I. B. Tauris)

GEORGE, DAVID R., and WAN SONYA TANG (eds). 2018. *Televising Restoration Spain: History and Fiction in Twenty-First-Century Costume Dramas* (Cham, Switzerland: Palgrave Macmillan)

GRANADA, EMILIANO. 2018. 'Movistar+ Original *Arde Madrid*'s Creators Open Up', *Variety*, 26 September <https://variety.com/2018/film/festivals/arde-madrid-movistar-original-creators-1202958259/> [accessed 21 February 2021]

HOPEWELL, JOHN. 1986. *Out of the Past: Spanish Cinema after Franco* (London: British Film Institute)

——. 2018. 'Movistar+ Expands its International Reach', *Variety*, 21 September <https:// variety.com/2018/tv/global/movistar-expands-global-reach-1202951384/> [accessed 21 February 2021]

—— and EMILIANO GRANADA. 2018. 'Movistar Plus' Drive into Fiction is Centered on Women', *Variety*, 15 October <https://variety.com/2018/tv/markets-festivals/movistar-plus-drive-into-fiction-centered-women-1202974241/> [accessed 21 February 2021]

LACALLE, CHARO, DEBORAH CASTRO, and MARILUZ SÁNCHEZ. 2014. 'Spain: The Boom of Fiction Set in the Past', in *Obitel 2014: Transmedia Production Strategies in Television Fiction* (Porto Alegre: Globo), pp. 267–308

OBITEL. 2015. *Gender Relations in Television Fiction* (Porto Alegre: Globo)

PALACIO, MANUEL. 2001. *Historia de la televisión en España* (Barcelona: Gedisa)

——. 2012. *La televisión durante la Transición española* (Madrid: Cátedra)

PARATI [*sic*]. 2019. 'Llega a nuestro país una serie con perspectiva feminista que es furor en Europa', *Infobae*, 5 May <https://www.infobae.com/parati/news/2019/05/05/llega-a-nuestro-pais-una-serie-con-perspectiva-feminista-que-es-furor-en-europa/> [accessed 21 February 2021]

PASTOR, CUSTODIO. 2018. 'Siguiendo a Ava Gardner en Madrid con Paco León', *El País*, 20 October <https://elpais.com/ccaa/2018/10/19/madrid/1539972575_043696.html> [accessed 21 February 2021]

PEIRÓ, PATRICIA. 2018. 'Feminismo de época' *El País*, 10 March <https://elpais.com/ cultura/2018/03/07/television/1520439416_387246.html?rel=mas> [accessed 21 February 2021]

POLASCHEK, BRONWYN. 2013. *The Post-Feminist Biopic* (Cham, Switzerland: Palgrave Macmillan)

RINCÓN, REYES. 2019. 'El Supremo concluye que La Manada actuó con pleno conocimiento de que la víctima no consintió', *El País*, 5 July <https://elpais.com/sociedad/2019/07/05/ actualidad/1562318324_192613.html> [accessed 21 February 2021]

RODERA, ALEJANDRO. 2018. 'Crítica de *Arde Madrid*: Paco León invade la España franquista con la revolución sexual', *FormulaTV*, 8 November <https://www.formulatv. com/noticias/critica-arde-madrid-paco-leon-invade-espana-franquista-revolucion-sexual-85627/> [accessed 21 February 2021]

RUIZ DE ELVIRA, ÁLVARO. 2018. '*La otra mirada*, las mujeres que necesita TVE', *El País*, 26 April <https://elpais.com/cultura/2018/04/25/television/1524667018_112619. html?rel=mas> [accessed 21 February 2021]

RUIZ MANTILLA, JESÚS. 2018. 'Paco León: "En mi familia, con una miga de pan se hace oro"', *El País*, 30 December <https://elpais.com/elpais/2018/12/28/gente/1546010583_870071. html> [accessed 21 February 2021]

SMITH, PAUL JULIAN. 2009. 'Transnational Telenovela: From Mexico to Madrid, via Barcelona', in *Spanish Screen Fiction: Between Cinema and Television*. (Liverpool: Liverpool University Press), pp. 122–44

——. 2016. 'Postcolonial TV: *El tiempo entre costuras*; *El Príncipe*', in *Dramatized Societies: Quality Television in Spain and Mexico* (Liverpool: Liverpool University Press), pp. 81–112

## References: Audiovisual

*Aída*. 2005–14. (Globomedia/Telecinco)

*Amar en tiempos revueltos*. 2005–present. (Diagonal/RTVE)

*Arde Madrid*. 2018. (Andy Joke/Movistar+)

*Carmina o revienta*. 2012. Dir. by Paco León (Andy Joke)

*Carmina y amén*. 2014. Dir. by Paco León (Andy Joke/Telecinco Cinema)

*Cuéntame cómo pasó*. 2001–present. Grupo Ganga/RTVE

*Gran Hotel*. 2011–13. (Bambú/Antena 3)

*otra mirada, La*. 2018–19. (Boomerang/RTVE)

*Kiki, el amor se hace*. 2016. Dir. by Paco León (Mediaset España)

*Paquita Salas*. 2016–present. (Flooxer/Neox/Netflix)

*tiempo entre costuras, El*. 2013–14. (Boomerang/Antena 3)

# CHAPTER 6

# From Madrid to California:
# Spanish Series in the Age of Netflix

### Spanish Production at the Digital Crossroads

On 4 September 2020 the *New York Times* ran a lengthy interview with Netflix CEO Reed Hastings by star columnist Maureen Dowd, who is more accustomed to profiling senior politicians than media moguls. Proclaiming him 'the man who killed Hollywood', Dowd also attacks old-school movie practices:

> After a long period when the club of mostly white, supposedly liberal men running Hollywood secured the power in a lockbox, keeping a death grip on the Academy of Motion Picture Arts and Sciences and acting shocked anew every time a movie with Asian or Black or female leads did great box office, Netflix is swiftly democratizing things.

As part of this 'democratization' Dowd lists a number of Netflix's original international titles including 'a Spanish period piece about phone operators'. This brief mention of drama series *Las chicas del cable* [Cable Girls] (2017–20), which had just posted its fifth and last season on the streaming platform, is the only reference to Spain in this long and prominently displayed piece. But the mention is, characteristically, in the context not of a discussion of Spanish media, culture, or language, but of a purely American debate over gender and ethnic diversity, one marked by the emergence in Hollywood of women or minority protagonists that were once held to be exceptional and anomalous. Indeed the piece is illustrated by stills from the British bio-series *The Crown* (whose protagonist is of course Queen Elizabeth) and the American *Barry* (whose subject is Barack Obama, the first African-American president).

On 4 October 2017 Netflix España had posted to its over one million subscribers on YouTube a short promotional video called 'Paquita Salas llega a Netflix' [Paquita Salas Comes to Netflix]. In it a plump, pink-suited Spanish matron walks boldly into the streamer's huge headquarters in Los Angeles, California. Confronting the bemused young receptionists, she tries out the only words of English she appears to know: 'meeting', 'telephone', and 'boss' (that boss would be the same Reed Hastings whom Maureen Dowd would interview so reverently three years later). The occasion is the adoption by Netflix (a name which Paquita struggles to pronounce as 'Neflis') of the second season of the eponymous Spanish comedy series, which had previously been seen only in Spain on the little-known web platform Flooxer and the minority cable channel Neox. As we saw in my first chapter, *Paquita Salas* (2016–), which now boasts three seasons, follows the very mixed fortunes of an unsuccessful talent agent based in Getafe, an unglamorous post-industrial town south of Madrid, which could not be further from flashy Silicon Valley. This culture clash is shown by means of linguistic facility, or rather lack of facility: the provincial Paquita's inability to master English. Much play is made in the series itself of its Spanish characters' problems in pronouncing such words as 'management' and 'hashtag'. And this short video continues and extends the Spanish series' deceptively simple genre of apparently improvisational comedy in a mockumentary format, parachuting it from everyday Getafe into a highly charged and exceptional American location.

The source of the humor in this short from the Spanish perspective is clear: it comes from a queasy embarrassment and self-deprecation embodied by an incompetent local representative of Spanish national media in the face of a highly successful global media phenomenon. Once inside Netflix's offices, in a further short video, Paquita fails to obtain her desired meeting with Hastings (saying she can't remember his name as it's 'a name in English'). She does however take greedy advantage of the free breakfast on offer and confidently misidentifies the American and British stars of Netflix's flagship series, such as *The Crown*, confusing them with more familiar (more familiar to Spaniards) Spanish actors.

The pleasure for a US audience in these short videos is less evident than it is for Spaniards, as is suggested by the apparently genuine befuddlement of the patient and polite Netflix workers Paquita encounters on her visit (the video has no English subtitles). And the question of diversity (or in Dowd's word 'democratization'), raised here in the confrontation of a Spanish-speaking visitor with native Anglo-Americans, soon shifts from nationality to gender and sexuality: as canny Spanish fans are well aware, the apparently middle-aged female protagonist Paquita is in fact played by a much younger gay man in drag, Brays Efe. It is a joke also lost on Netflix's unfortunate receptionists.

As these two anecdotes suggest, in the face of a constant deluge of content it is not easy to identify the US point of view on rare Spanish shows. Netflix keeps its famous algorithm, which identifies preferences and recommends choices to individual subscribers, fiercely private, interested as it is in preserving and expanding its accounts, rather than promoting brute numbers of viewership for single titles. And recently the streamer shifted to a criterion of just two minutes' watching as a measure of what counts as a 'view' (Elfring 2020), suggesting an at best tangential interest by households in single shows, even in figures that remain private to the company.

In spite of requests to Netflix's press office, I received no information on figures for the US audience for Spanish series, much less more detailed data on the demographic segments that Netflix must surely have, broken down as they would be by gender and language. The Spanish originals can be seen with subtitles or dubbed, a resource Netflix takes with a seriousness unaccustomed in the US. And it is impossible to know if series made in Spain are promoting knowledge of the

Spanish language in the US, as Anglophone viewers may be watching the content in dubbed versions or, if not, may well be Spanish speakers already themselves (the Latinx community in the US, whose linguistic ability is of course variable in both Spanish and English, is now the largest minority in the country).

Anecdotally, Netflix's Spanish titles provoke unusual interest in Latin America. For example, before the pandemic, I observed how pirate DVD sets of *La casa de papel* [Money Heist] (2017–) were put on prominent display by street vendors in Mexico City. This suggests a new taste for Spanish fare by low-income Mexican audiences who lack high-speed internet at home and have never had access to such series on their accustomed free-to-air television service. The same may well hold true for US Latinx, previously limited to broadcast networks Telemundo and Univision and their overwhelmingly Mexican telenovelas.

Traditionally there has been strong mass resistance to both subtitling and dubbing in English-language territories such as the US. 'Foreign-language film' is a synonym for minority 'specialist' or 'art' movies and has, as a niche genre, long been exiled to a small number of specialist movie theaters. From the 1980s US independent directors took over from foreign auteurs even in those theaters. And foreign-language series have always been wholly absent from broadcast and basic cable TV in the USA.

But more recently this lack of interest has cut both ways, in television at least. When an Italian scholar like Milly Buonanno speaks of a 'transatlantic romance', she speaks of European critics and scholars enamored of the current second golden age of American TV (2014). However general audiences in Europe or Latin America are not so impressed by this boundary-pushing fare, as US series are exiled to marginal time slots on free-to-air television and minority channels on cable. Around the world the preference is now for local production whose cultural closeness guarantees a pleasurable cultural premium to local viewers.

Moreover 'format translations' (or remakes) tend to travel as much from Europe to the US as they do in the other direction. Spanish and Catalan titles such as *Los misterios de Laura* [The Mysteries of Laura] (TVE, 2009–14) and *Polseres vermelles* [The Red Band Society] (TV3, 2011–13) were recently remade, albeit to little success, for the US broadcast networks (as indeed was the Mexican *Mujeres asesinas* [Killer Women] (Televisa, 2008–10)). Even before the rise of Netflix, the television ecology was far from that of the 1980s, when American mainstream dramas like *Dallas* (CBS, 1978–91) were dubbed for mass broadcast in prime time in territories around the globe. The multipolar world that followed the *Dallas* era, one that existed well before streaming, is documented in scholarly books such as *Global Television Formats*, which refutes the old cultural imperialism hypothesis of overwhelming media Americanization (Oren and Shahaf 2012).

Netflix rarely volunteers the national origin of content before the casual viewer clicks on it. Indeed its interface actively hides foreign-language titles even to those who seek them: it took me months to discover that *Fariña* (Bambú/Antena 3, 2018), an acclaimed series on drug smuggling in Galicia, was available in the US under the title *Cocaine Coast*, as the algorithm did not see fit to recommend it to me. *Money Heist* remains a shockingly banal translation of the enigmatic and evocative

FIG. 6.1. The four female leads of prison drama *Vis a Vis*. From left: La Rizos (Berta Vázquez), Macarena (Maggie Civantos), Zulema (Najwa Nimri), and Saray (Alba Flores)

original name *La casa de papel*. The same goes for the generic name assigned to *Vis a vis* (Globomedia/Antena 3, 2015–19): *Locked Up*. There is clearly a cultural deficit in the loss of idiomatic flavor in titles, as well as in dubbed dialogue, a loss which is invisible or inaudible to English speakers.

When I actively search for 'Spanish series' at home in New York City, an activity which relatively few English speakers with Netflix subscriptions are likely to contemplate, I am often rewarded with Mexican titles, of which more later. Of course this coincides with the linguistic usage of everyday life in the US where bodegas (minimarkets) advertising 'Spanish food' stock items such as *nopales* and refried beans.

Evidence for the US reception of Spanish series (or, rather, series from Spain) is limited and derives from three sources:

1. The trade or specialist press, such as the venerable *Variety* and the more sprightly *Hollywood Reporter*. This coverage is divided between specialist journalists, long located in Spain and highly knowledgeable of the local scene; and generalists, based in Los Angeles, whose responsibility is to the US industry as their sole audience.

2. The general press (especially the *New York Times*). This offers brief reviews guiding readers through the labyrinth of streaming platforms which has recently taken the place of the programming grid that the *Times* stopped publishing only in August 2020. As cultural gate keepers, the main newspapers retain some prestige and influence amongst elite audiences who are likely to have some interest in foreign-language fare.

FIG. 6.2. The four female leads of costume drama *Las chicas del cable*.
From left: Marga (Nadia de Santiago), Ángeles (Maggie Civantos),
Lidia (Blanca Suárez), Carlota (Ana Fernández)

3. Social media, such as Twitter. Only the most committed fans post here. While it is easy to identify English-language commentary on, say, discrete media events such as the finale of *Las chicas del cable*, it is difficult to establish the geographical origin of the posters, as this information (along with a real name) is not required by the platform. And of course Spanish-language tweets may well come from viewers in the US; and English-language tweets from Spanish-speaking territories.

Even given these limited and problematic sources, it would appear that Spanish-produced titles do favor female protagonists and female audiences. A search at my home for 'Spanish TV shows' on 7 September 2020, biased of course toward the algorithm's anticipation of my own preferences, gave the following results, according to Netflix's various official categories, all given in their translated English titles: on the main banner was period romance *Gran Hotel* [Grand Hotel] (2011–13); under 'popular' came: *Alta mar* [High Seas] (2019–20), *Gran Hotel*, *Velvet* (2013–16), *Valeria* (2020), *Las chicas del cable*; under 'ensemble': *Merlí* (2015–18), *Tiempos de guerra* [Morocco: Love in Times of War] (2017), *45 RPM* (2019); and finally under 'Netflix originals': *Paquita Salas* (which, as we saw, actually originated on a Spanish internet platform and cable channel), *Tiempos de guerra* (first made for Antena 3, the Spanish free-to-air network), *Alta mar*, *Valeria*, and *La casa de papel*. Most of these series are female-led, albeit boasting handsome male co-stars (see Yon González in romances *Gran Hotel* and *Las chicas del cable*); and only three are set in the present day (see Catalan high-school drama *Merlí*, female buddy sex comedy *Valeria*, and mockumentary *Paquita Salas* once more, a title which is nonetheless, as I we saw in Chapter 1, closely concerned with television history).

In this range of titles, then, there seems to be a correspondence between gender and genre. The many costume dramas boast lavish wardrobes and attractively varied set designs, even in a military hospital in the 1920s (*Tiempos de guerra*), on a trans-Atlantic ship in the 1940s (*Alta mar*), or in the music industry in the 1960s (*45 RPM*). Finally most of these female-led, period dramas are also listed by Netflix as 'ensemble' pieces. Even when, rarely, a contemporary title cites a single character (*Valeria*, *Paquita*), the emphasis is on the supportive relationships and dramatic conflicts within a mainly female collective (the faithful group of single friends of *Valeria*, which is highly reminiscent of the foursome in HBO's *Sex and the City* (1998–2004); the less faithful roster of female actors clients of *Paquita*).

Do these criteria, exhibited by a range of Spanish series currently on Netflix, constitute competitive advantages for Spanish creators on the platform? After all, showrunners around the world pitch innumerable concepts to Ted Sarandos, the streamer's head of content, who Reed Hastings himself identifies in Dowd's interview as the 'heart' of the company. It seems fair to say that in very broad terms US television production, although huge and diverse, is, unlike the Spanish, contemporary and male-biased. For many years the broadcast networks have relied heavily on the legal procedural genre which has spawned so many franchises, such as the multiple *Law & Orders* and *CSIs*. The main role for women here is as victims of gruesome murders. Indeed the *Washington Post* satirized this tendency as recently as 2018, when humorist Alexandra Petri wrote, as a controversial network CEO left in disgrace, of 'one of the many women whose stories CBS told': 'Nameless Nude Female Corpse'.

Beyond the fading but still powerful broadcast networks with their formulaic, anti-feminist genres, prestige cable channels have broken through in recent decades with series focusing on 'difficult men'. As we saw in Chapter 3, the book of that same name by Brett Martin in 2013 traced connections between their ambivalent anti-hero protagonists and their newly celebrated but troubled showrunners. Classic titles are of course *The Sopranos* (HBO, 1999–2007), *Mad Men* (AMC, 2007–15), and *Breaking Bad* (AMC, 2008–13). TV critic Emily Nussbaum asked where the 'difficult women' were on American TV, the female Tony Sopranos and Walter Whites? (cited in Buonanno 2017: 8). Moreover, relatively absent in US programming, both everyday and quality, is a female-skewed genre common in Europe (and especially in Spain), in film as on TV: costume drama. *Mad Men* dressed its female supporting players in gorgeous 1960s outfits, but its main attraction was surely the trials and triumphs of the male protagonist, Don Draper.

The social protest movement known as #MeToo, which has had relatively little impact in Spain, focused at first in the US media industry on a single sexually predatory executive: Harvey Weinstein. His production company Miramax specialized in premium movies with, ironically enough, a bias towards that female-skewed genre, the period picture. But #MeToo also called belated and increased attention to long-lasting research projects on gender discrimination in Hollywood, such as that led by veteran actor Geena Davis with her 'Institute on Gender and Media' (2020). These provided full data for the underrepresentation of women in US media at all levels: as actor-protagonists, directors, and producers.

However, the analysis of gender exclusion also immediately invoked in a US context intersectionality, that is, the way in which multiple categories of marginalization reinforce one another (compare Dowd's reference to 'Black, Asian, and female leads'). And parallel projects were equally visible for 'rewriting the script of LGBTQ' representation (GLAAD: which has a Spanish-language prize for queer characters (2020)); and for ethnic minorities (especially in relation to the Academy, also cited by Dowd). Such research projects had long examined not just the quantity but also the quality of images. In September 2020 the Oscar nominations finally instituted new diversity rules based on intersectional criteria that required the inclusion of women, LGBTQ people, ethnic minorities, and the differently abled in front of and behind the camera for feature films to qualify for awards (Buchanan 2020).

On a smaller scale we might compare the controversy, also in 2020, over the Criterion Collection. An American art and auteur movie DVD and streaming imprint, which boasts several classic Spanish-language titles such as Erice's *El espíritu de la colmena* [The Spirit of the Beehive] (Víctor Erice, 1973), Criterion focuses on foreign film otherwise inaccessible in the US and hosts a broad selection of work by female directors. Yet it was still attacked by the *New York Times* for featuring very little African-American work (Buchanan and Ugwu 2020). It is also telling that the Presidency of Donald Trump began in 2016 with massive demonstrations by women, many in iconic pussy hats. By summer 2020, however, as new elections approached, social protest was mainly spearheaded by Black Lives Matter. It is thus impossible to think the issues of gender and race separately in a US context.

Anecdotally, as we have said, the highest profile Netflix series from Spain appear to be costume dramas with female protagonists that skew to a female audience (I have called attention to this genre in previous chapters of this book). Yet I know of no book-length study of such works. As a control for the case of Spain, we might briefly return to Mexico. Scholar Guillermo Orozco (2020) has edited a lengthy collection of essays on series made for the streamer in this second-largest Spanish-language market titled *Televisión en tiempos de Netflix: una nueva oferta mediática* [Television in Times of Netflix: A New Media Supply]. Orozco and his colleagues do not confirm for Mexico the female bias found in Spain or the focus on period or costume drama. Two essays in the volume are on heavily male narco-dramas and one on the 'disappearance of women' in a successful bio-series on singer Luis Miguel. The one chapter devoted to female characters in Netflix's Mexican series, all set in the present, claims that they fit into traditional stereotypes of good and bad women: mother, trophy wife etc. (2020: 116).

An earlier scholarly article on Netflix in Mexico by Margarita Cornelio-Marí (2020) claims that the platform 'localizes' its content made in that country through the appeal to elements of the Mexican genre of melodrama (a supposed female favorite) and the artistic heritage of the nation's classic film. These are elements likely to be accessible only to local audiences. And we might ask if the same process holds true for the platform's Spanish productions, in this case via Netflix's appeal to a genre of female-centered costume drama already existing on broadcast TV.

There are indeed connections between markets under Netflix's aegis. In a flagrant example of cross-promotion, in another short film the globe-trotting Paquita Salas visits not California but Mexico City. There she encounters, to her delight, Paco León of *Arde Madrid*, a Spanish actor featured in a Mexican series, also female-led. *La Casa de las Flores* [The House of Flowers] (2018–20) is a flamboyant parody of traditional telenovela with a transgender theme that parallels *Paquita Salas'* transvestite comedy. And it is set in both Mexico and Spain.

Netflix has based its European operation in Spain and has built its extensive studios, known as Content City, outside Madrid. Beyond Latin America, the streamer thus clearly has a special interest in the country. In the rest of this chapter I offer a close reading of three case studies, of series made in Spain and shown in the US. I place them on a continuum or, rather, two continuums: from the most to the least Spanish, that is, making reference to Spain and its history and inscribed in the conventions of Spanish TV drama; and from the most to the least female, that is cast with women actors, addressed to women viewers, and inscribed in the conventions of TV genres conventionally gendered as feminine.

One proviso should be made. Some of the most explicitly feminist and historical of recent Spanish broadcast series are unseen on US streaming, perhaps because of the cultural deficit resulting from a plethora of local references or from simple lack of transmission rights from the state broadcaster. Time-travel drama *El Ministerio del Tiempo* [The Ministry of Time] (TVE, 2015–), treated in Chapter 2 of this book, rewrites Spanish history in a feminine key (its creators successfully sued the US producers of a similar show for plagiarism); and period high-school drama *La otra mirada* [A Different View] (TVE, 2018–19), treated in Chapter 5, rewrites the 1920s via contemporary incidents, notably the savage gang rape of a young girl by a group of men known as the wolf pack or *manada*. This event took place in 2016 but was recreated in the series' period setting in 2018, the same year in which the real-life perpetrators were first tried, thus showing the 'presentism' of costume drama sometimes dismissed as simple nostalgia. Both series also featured convincing and moving lesbian characters that would have been appreciated by US audiences sensitive to intersectionality, had they had the chance to see them.

Moreover local streaming services, which grew out of free-to-air national channels, rival Netflix in their artistic and popular reach: the Javis' *Veneno* may be distributed by HBO Max in the US, but it was first seen on Atresmedia's premium service in Spain. And Atresmedia's groundbreaking *Arde Madrid*, studied in Chapter 5, remains unavailable in the USA.

## Three Case Studies of Female-Centered Series in Spain

My three examples of Spanish fiction series that did make it to Netflix's US platform are: *Vis a vis*, from Globomedia and Antena 3, a women's prison drama that boasts both a female ensemble cast and central identification character; *Las chicas del cable*, a period romance also with a female ensemble cast, from Bambú and Antena 3, also; and *La casa de papel*, a heist thriller with a mixed-gender cast and, arguably, a female protagonist, which is promoted as a genuine Netflix original (a problematic term). This last series belongs to a genre unknown in Spain. And although *La casa de papel* (like *Vis a vis*) appeared only in last position when I made my search for 'Spanish series' from my home in New York City, it is widely held to be the most popular foreign-language title ever streamed on Netflix. While only *Las chicas del cable* is set in the past, the two other contemporary series have much in common with it, both artistically and commercially.

In analyzing these three titles I will draw briefly on three critical commentaries: respectively, a book length study edited by Milly Buonanno on the 'bad girls' of global television in the crime genre, who have succeeded the 'difficult men' of the recent earlier era (2017); another scholarly volume on Spanish period drama of the Restoration, which places *Las chicas del cable* in the context of its free to air TV predecessors (George and Tang 2018); and Netflix's own documentary on *La casa de papel* (2020), which examines the Spanish series as a global phenomenon. In general we should add, however, that there is an increase in budgets over successive seasons (especially in my second and third examples), which permits more exterior and international shooting, thus somewhat distancing the drama and its audience from the original Spanish context and locations.

The international success of such series did not appear likely given the unique distinguishing characteristics of Spanish series in their home environment, many of which were surely unwelcome on the international streaming medium. Spanish series have until very recently employed lengthy episodes of well over an hour, stretching to two hours with commercial breaks. These far exceeded the international US standard of some 40–50 minutes, inherited from the 60 minute slots of commercial network grids. And taking up the whole evening and running until 1 a.m. in their home markets, Spanish series required larger casts and more intricate plotlines to hold the attention of their patient viewers than their brisker US equivalents. Spanish series also tended to mix the genres of drama and comedy which the US system kept separate, aiming as the Spaniards did to attract a broad family audience for the whole evening.

The period genre, more common in Spain than in the US, also requires a passing knowledge of Spanish history of its audience, even in titles that take place in hermetic locations like the eponymous *Gran Hotel* or the transatlantic liner in *Alta mar*. Spanish drama also appealed to the country's established star system, with actors familiar to local audiences from film and TV, whether youthful (Blanca Suárez in *Las chicas del cable*) or veteran (Concha Velasco in *Gran Hotel*). These cast members were barely known to international viewers. There is some evidence that Netflix subsequently attempted to extend this Spanish star system to the US in its later original titles. For example, a press release in August 2020 for *Jaguar*, a forthcoming series on Nazi war criminals in Francoist Spain (a concept unlikely to be familiar to US audiences), is said to be 'the new series with Blanca Suárez' (About Netflix 2020).

Finally and crucially, recent Spanish dramas appeal to concrete locations in the Peninsula. As Concepción Cascajosa wrote, where once they seemed to take place in a vague 'series planet', now they were set in places recognizable to Spanish audiences, often in the regions (2016: 24). There is a parallel with tone and content here. Spanish networks traditionally sought the least-objectionable shows, those which would provoke no complaints from 'la señora de Cuenca' [the lady from Cuenca] (a proverbial figure representing a conservative provincial viewer). Now specificity of place is combined with boundary-pushing premises: one example here is the previously mentioned Galician drug-smuggling drama, *Fariña*, which surely did not appeal to the conservative Spanish ladies who favored undemanding family viewing.

While all these tendencies might seem to alienate international audiences, especially in the United States where viewers are most likely to be unfamiliar with the history and geography of Spain, they also testified to the professionalism and virtuosity of long-lasting producers (such as Álex Pina, who would create *La casa de papel*) and production companies (Globomedia, which pivoted from family-friendly dramedies and historical romances such as *Águila roja* [Red Eagle] (2009–16) to the brutal contemporary prison drama *Vis a vis*). Meanwhile some companies specialized, creating lengthy and lucrative track records, as in the case of Bambú which favored expert female-targeted costume drama. Hence, while the formal properties of Spanish series, such as the extended episode length, were alien to US audiences, the industrial proficiency of Spanish companies was welcome to a new and inexperienced entrant to the American and global market, such as Netflix.

## American Reception

At the end of this chapter I will offer an analysis of single episodes from my three series, from an assumed US perspective (this must of course be tentative and impressionistic for such a large and diverse country). First, however, I will treat the relatively limited US specialized and general press and social media coverage of series from Spain, as it offers some valuable evidence for reception. Unsurprisingly, perhaps, this coverage exhibits twin tensions between the national and the international and between the female and the universal.

Thus in February 2019 *Variety* wrote that 'Netflix unveil[ed] five new Spanish original series' on the eve of the Berlin Film Festival, where its first movie ever playing in competition was also by a Spanish or Catalan woman director (Isabel Coixet helmed *Elisa & Marcela*) (Hopewell and Lang 2019a). Distinguished Spanish specialist John Hopewell and his colleague describe these new TV titles in wholly Spanish terms: *Días de navidad* [Three Days of Christmas] (2019), a historical drama on four sisters celebrating Christmas over successive years and decades, is said to be directed by Pau Freixas of the previously mentioned Catalan series *Polseres vermelles*; the lead writer of *Valeria* is María López Castaño, said to have come from *Gran Hotel*.

Netflix's vice president for original series, however, claims 'We want to produce local stories with a global appeal'. And he cites *La casa de papel* as 'the most watched foreign series' ever on Netflix; and high-school drama *Elite*, as ranked by one audience measurement company, as 'the most watched series in the world during parts of October'. Hopewell comments that the new series 'see the streaming giant still predominantly targeting women and YA [young adult] viewers'. It was an audience invoked two years earlier, also in Berlin, by the producer and showrunner of *Las chicas del cable*, Teresa Fernández Valdés: 'What I think we can offer Netflix is a story mainly directed at woman [*sic*]' (Roxborough 2017). She continues: 'It isn't just the female audience we are targeting, but women, strong women, are the protagonists of the series'.

The opposite point of view to that of Hopewell's is shown in a preview of *Elite* which presents the Spanish high-school drama wholly within the optic of US expectations. In 'Netflix's Elite Subverts Teen Drama Tropes with Style', non-specialist Caroline Framke (2018) compares the show to three earlier American ones ('*The OC* multiplied by *Gossip Girl* divided by *Laura Mars*') and identifies 'three classic storylines' familiar from these American teen dramas (the rich rebel, the jerk with a heart of gold, and the steamy love triangle). Praising the intersectional element, which is of course the holy grail for American media, the journalist highlights the presence in the ensemble cast of a poor Muslim female student.

Framke does not inform *Variety*'s readers, and perhaps does not know, that Carlos Montero, *Elite*'s showrunner, had previously created a very similar network high school show, *Física o química* [Physics or Chemistry] (Antena 3, 2008–11). But, interestingly, she does advise American viewers to 'select the original "European Spanish" as the overdub with English subtitles' as Netflix will otherwise default to 'a distracting English dub'. This is rare evidence that a Spanish series can actively promote the Spanish language for English speakers in the US.

Most interesting are articles on late seasons of long-lasting Spanish series, by Hopewell once more (2020). Now he examines how the streaming giant and the genre of the Spanish series have evolved in parallel, as the country had become Netflix's official European production 'hub'. Thus Season 5 of *Las chicas del cable*, which premiered in February 2020, was acclaimed 'the third most binged SVOD [subscription video on demand] series in the world over its first week of release' (figures are attributed to trade resource *TV Time*, not the cagy Netflix itself). This streaming series is built on the period genre its production company Bambú had pioneered on terrestrial television, given here as 'romantic melodrama'. Hopewell cites the promotion of Peninsular Spanish language here not in the US, but in Latin America: Bambú's *Gran Hotel* and *Velvet* were the first to be shown in the continent 'without being dubbed into so-called neutral Spanish'.

Evidence for the parallel growth of the streamer and of the series are: the 'opening up to exteriors' beyond the first season's studio sets; 'ratcheting up the action' with the final season featuring Civil War battle action; 'priming gender issues', with the third season focusing on a lesbian affair (one media analyst based in London tells us 'race, gender, and sexuality are all very, very hot at the moment'); and finally 'Netflix [as] a needed local player'. While the first season was greenlit out of Los Angeles, the last, we are told, was produced directly from Madrid. Even as, we are told, 'Netflix is moving toward more broad audience demographics' (those battle scenes are intended to appeal to new male viewers), *Las chicas del cable* became more

FIG. 6.3. Úrsula Corberó as female lead Tokyo in action drama *La casa de papel*

strongly female, even feminist ('the girls set out to fight for all the women in Spain, as a reflection of the rest of the world') and more Spanish (it was now wholly planned and made in Madrid and focused on great events in the nation's history).

The premiere of the third series of *La casa de papel* raises similar questions. Interviewing showrunner Álex Pina, Hopewell and his colleague make once more some general observations (Hopewell and Lang 2019b). First comes the much bigger budget, perhaps the biggest ever spent in Spain. Where once the show was set within the confines of Madrid's Bank of Spain headquarters, now it features locations as diverse as its characters' pseudonyms (the female narrator-protagonist is called Tokyo): Panama, Argentina, Florence, and Java. Secondly the series is now a 'feminist actioner', with Tokyo claiming her right to sexual freedom even within a steady romantic relationship.

Thirdly, its characters, timeframes, and narrative structures are now more complex. Hopewell even appeals to literary modernism as a model for the series' increasing formal experimentation.

Finally Pina says in this article that *La casa de papel* is 'Latino and proud of it', a relatively rare comment for a Spaniard. While he concedes that the heist genre is 'Anglo-Saxon', his series, he continues, offers 'greater affective dynamics', that is, the more intense emotions that are thought to be typically Latin. But while Pina stresses the world's 700 million Spanish-speakers, Hopewell identifies rather rare

Peninsular idioms that give the dialogue its flavor. These include 'Al solomillo', which he translates as 'Get to the steak part of the menu'. He does not mention, but certainly knows, that the character Tokyo who pronounces this phrase is played by Úrsula Corberó, the Catalan actor who came to fame in broadcast series *Física o química*, mentioned earlier. This is a casting choice that is familiar to and enjoyed by only Spanish viewers (Corberó also plays a cameo as a version of herself, a newly successful international actor nostalgic for her more modest Spanish TV origins, in the third season of *Paquita Salas*).

Clearly the producers and actors featured in the trade publications desire the broadest audience possible for their series, even as they appeal to distinct gender and national profiles in those series as part of a brutal struggle for competitive advantage with rival content from around the world. And this tendency is confirmed by brief notices in the US general press, anxious to promote little-known foreign-language titles to their elite readers as a sign of distinctive taste amongst the new deluge of TV titles.

The assumed time pressure on busy readers is suggested by the *New York Times'* critic's regular column 'How Much Watching Time Do You Have This Weekend?' On 4 May 2017 Margaret Lyons recommends *Las chicas del cable* 'if you have a few hours and love jaunty hats'. In a brief account of what is called 'a Spanish melodrama' (a term Lyons is unlikely to use to describe a US series) the emphasis here is on period wardrobe, a stereotypically female preoccupation: 'hats, bob haircuts and drop waist dresses abound'. The plot is described as 'dreams, romance, safe cracking, vermouth, and lots of longing glances'. And this high-budget, quality series is described, dismissively once more, as a 'soap'. The critic warns readers in a way that suggests they may be put off by its national origin: 'It's in Spanish, but is available subtitled and dubbed'.

Two years later American audiences are thought to have changed. In 'The Thirty Best International TV Shows of the Decade' (run on 20 December 2019) Mike Hale celebrates 'the explosion of global content that came to American screens'. He also comments on the language question: 'Americans *will* read subtitles, it turns out. (I'd prefer to think no one's choosing the dubbed English soundtracks.)' The only Spanish title here is *La casa de papel*, somewhat dismissively compared in Spanglish to an American movie director: 'en el estilo de Quentin Tarantino [*sic*]. Here the focus is on the narrative innovation cited by Hopewell: 'this puzzle box of a series employs time trickery, unreliable narration, [and] flashy graphics'. There is no mention of female agency or audience here. Nor is there when the series breaks out of the 'international' ghetto to be included in another regular feature, 'The Best 50 TV Shows on Netflix Now' (Murray). Described on 8 September 2020 as a 'hyperkinetic Spanish action-adventure', *La casa de papel* is acclaimed as 'one of the rare foreign television series to find a big and appreciative audience in the United States'.

What is striking, then, is that these two series, the only ones mentioned in the paper of record for cultured liberal readers, would appear to have so little in common, in terms of either gender or genre. Unlike for Netflix itself and for the more informed trade press, 'Spanishness' and 'femaleness' are not seen as criteria that offer a competitive advantage.

What, then, do viewers themselves make of the series? It is well known that Spanish fans of *Vis a vis*, known as the 'Yellow Horde' after the distinctive costumes of the prison inmates, kept the series alive as it transferred from Spanish broadcaster Antena 3 to global streamer Netflix via Fox Spain. The most interesting and accessible evidence for US fandom, however, comes from the response to the climactic final season of *Las chicas del cable*.

Netflix tries to corral English-speaking tweets on the series with @CableGirlsNet. But real commentary is much more diverse than the streamer intends. Some viewers offer lists of favorite broadcast shows where *Las chicas del cable* is the only foreign or, indeed, historical title, suggesting Netflix has indeed broken through to new English-speaking audiences (I have not corrected grammar, punctuation, and spelling in the following quotes): 'the good place, brooklyn 99, cable girls, friends, the walking dead...'. (@hoesgtg, 9 September 2020). Others focus on make-up, bringing costume drama into the present: 'What color is the lipstick the actress who plays Lidia Aguilar...? I think it would work on me' (@suzannejbennett, 10 September 2020).

Still others attest on the contrary to a deep emotional engagement with the series and an intense identification with its characters: 'I waited two months to watch the final episodes [...] to avoid how emotional I would feel knowing this would be the end of the road with our #CableGirls' (@tarabitran, 10 September 2020). Yet others run with the series' avowed feminist messaging, perhaps further than the creators intended: 'Dude I've been watching cable girls all day and GOD knows how much I despise men now' (@fatherfunker9, 4 September 2020). Or again 'i was in a gc [group chat] and i liked because we are all women but then there is an ugly man talking bad about cable girls. i hate men can they just die or something' (@saintchnel, 10 September 2020). Clearly the series' period setting was no barrier to audience pleasure and identification.

Further commentary suggests the series can serve as a focus of intersectionality, that special goal of US seekers of diversity. Tweeters identifying themselves as Black women offer highly idiomatic praise, in an attempt to create a distinctive community of fans: 'But nah fr... [*sic*] Ya'll gotta watch Cable Girls' (@ixxieee, 5 September 2020); or again 'i was skeptical about cable girls but since you recommend it i'll watch. thanks boo!' (@jawmss, 8 September 2020). More rarely, English-speakers directly address the question of language learning: 'convincing myself I'm studying by watching Spanish tv shows "brushing up on my Spanish" [...] olé'; and 'ok now i'm crying at cable girls, like honestly it's SO GOOD, even if you don't speak Spanish you should watch it with English subtitles' (@elipollylu, both tweets 11 September 2020). Or again and more explicitly: 'told my spanish professor i want to learn the language bc it's useful professionally but it's really so i can understand the cable girls' cast's interviews' (@riomattoo, 7 September 2020).

More generally Twitter attests to how English-speaking audiences, overwhelmingly female, integrate the successive seasons of the series into their lives. For example

@vallery18477937 tweets a grid of four images. At the top are the lovers played by Blanca Suárez and Yon González as they appear, young, innocent, and enamored in the hopeful pilot; at the bottom the same actors, older and distraught in the tragic finale. The user's commentary is simple: 'The first time and the last time'. The words are reinforced by weeping face and heart emojis (4 September 2020). There is a sense of history here not only in the period setting of the series but in the lengthy duration of its production and consumption.

We have seen that the trade press explains national references or international parallels to a professional audience and the general press recommends the superficial pleasures of wardrobe and plot to its busy readers. In spite of its reputation for vapid triviality, social media attests rather to the immersive affective experience of female fan communities of *Las chicas del cable*, one which may even lead some to explore the original language of favorite characters they cannot bear to lose intimate media contact with.

## Opening Episodes

Milly Buonanno's previously mentioned book *Television Antiheroines: Women Behaving Badly in Crime and Prison Drama* charts the rise of bad girls in global series of the last decade. These 'strong female leads' offer 'dark sides of human personality and behavior, moral ambiguity, damaging flaws [and] enduring strength', equal to those of TV's earlier 'difficult men' (2017: 4). Buonanno does not mention *Vis a vis*, but Globomedia's production for Antena 3, later taken over by Netflix, fulfills her challenging criteria. And while the protagonist Macarena, the stereotypical naive new inmate, is white, the rest of the female ensemble is unusually diverse for Spain, boasting previously unknown black and Roma actors.

Co-star Najwa Nimri, as Zulema, in real life of Basque and Jordanian descent, is given some dialogue in Arabic. A central and dignified focus on lesbian relationships amongst the women hits the spot for intersectionality also.

Yet *Vis a vis* should not be seen as a successor to Netflix's American women in prison drama *Orange Is the New Black* (2013–19), which also featured ethnic and gender diversity. Indeed Globomedia's Álex Pina, soon to strike out on his own with *La casa de papel*, explicitly cites *Vis a vis*'s resistance to US 'colonization' and refusal to follow American models (Smith 2019: 69). And the first episode offers many distinctively Spanish touches, beginning with its extended length of 74 minutes (some 30 minutes longer than typical American series), its large ensemble cast, and intricate plotlines: the innocent Macarena's conflicts with her new companions are crosscut with the story of her betrayal by the embezzling boyfriend-boss who put her behind bars and the search for a nine million euro booty stolen in an armed robbery.

Netflix's English title for the pilot of *Vis a vis* is 'Dead Mosquito'. This is a botched literal translation of the Spanish idiom 'mosquita muerta', which refers to a deceptively meek person 'who wouldn't hurt a fly'. It corresponds to protagonist Macarena's series arc from ingénue to hard-bitten inmate. In the pre-credit sequence the blonde heroine releases a pet canary, whose yellow will rhyme with the signature uniforms of the prisoners, from a high-rise apartment. It is a location that reads as 'wealthy big city' to US viewers, but is readily recognizable as Madrid's historic Gran Vía to Spaniards. There is thus from the beginning a significant loss of meaning, both verbal and spatial, for US viewers.

The series is, however, clearly addressed from the start to a female demographic: the opening phone call to Macarena's mother that plays over this sequence establishes relations between women as a focus of drama credits (the father does not appear until later). And as Macarena enters the prison for the first time, she is observed by a skeptical inmate with a large Afro hairstyle (called by the guard 'Rizos' [Curly]). This signals familiarity to a US audience that prizes the ethnic diversity of *Orange Is the New Black*. But the strip-search that follows shows frontal nudity just six minutes in, challenging more prudish US sensibilities.

Female physicality is also highly stressed throughout this first episode: the protagonist is menstruating as she is roughly examined with a gloved hand. Later a female guard pumps breast milk, shown in close-up. The original Spanish language is as graphic as the image, featuring crude lesbian sex references from established inmates. Pseudo-documentary interviews, shot straight to camera and with jump cuts, reinforce the challenging realism of the show. Moreover regional and, especially, class differences that are marked in the original Spanish dialogue (Macarena is a middle-class girl from 'central Madrid' surrounded by deprived women from the slums) are lost to Americans listening to the English dub.

*Las chicas del cable*, devised from the start for an international audience, looks and sounds very different. As David R. George and Wan Sonya Tang's book demonstrates, it takes up its place in Spain in the context of a large number of previous series on this period of the Restoration, held to be a relatively happy period before the horrors of the Civil War and Dictatorship. Most are made, as here, by Bambú, but shown on broadcast network Antena 3. It is a historical periodization that is of course unknown to the American audience. The episode title here is the bland 'Dreams' (easily translated from the Spanish 'Sueños') and its length is a brisk international standard of 53 minutes, also signaling conformity with the preferences of the US spectator.

The pre-credit sequence features voice-over from protagonist Alba (a glamorous Blanca Suárez shown here at a fancy party), which is excessively explicit on feminism and women's position in the period. Alba solemnly declaims that in 1928 women were just decorative and their dream of freedom seemed impossible. This text serves to 'place' the US viewer and connect with the young contemporary female audience (compare the use of an anachronistic modern music track with English lyrics throughout the series). This opening is much more literal than *Vis a vis*'s more subtle appeal to class and ethnicity in Spain, because it was intended, once more, to be clicked on by the international (American) public. Moreover voice-over is in itself a reassuring technique for the new viewer that is absent in the more challenging prison drama.

This opening voice-over is set to a quick cut montage of future central characters suffering from macho violence. Alba's three sidekicks are Ángeles, a downtrodden, brutalized wife (played by the same actor who starred in *Vis a vis*); Carlota, a wealthy daughter, her options limited by her patriarchal father; and Marga, a timid country girl leaving her stifling village and family for a taste of freedom in the big city. The swift exposition and establishment of characters are in a familiar American pace, not the extended rhythm previously favored by more leisurely Spanish series.

In the first shot of the episode proper, Alma is shown in cloche hat and raspberry lipstick that matches her day dress (we remember American critics drew attention to the series' expert wardrobe and American fans on Twitter to its desirable cosmetics). Alma is placed in a meticulous digital reconstruction of Madrid's Gran Vía in the 1920s, including what she calls a 'new skyscraper'. This is very reminiscent of the real-life iconic Telefónica building, even though the architecture and the company's name have been slightly changed ('Telefonía'). This was the only avenue in Madrid comparable to New York or Chicago in the period and was indeed partly inspired by their example. It is thus a setting readily accessible to American audiences. We should compare *Vis a vis*'s understated use of the same location, the Gran Vía, which is bluntly explained by voice-over in *Las chicas del cable*.

Entering the glamorous art deco lobby from the street with the as yet unknown romantic male lead, the executive played by Yon González (previously of *Gran Hotel*), smart and sly Alma steals another candidate's identity and presents herself as one of many women competing for prized jobs at the company. She will later cheat on the typing test and flirt with one of the managers to ensure she is taken on. Alma, an experienced safe-breaker, is thus one of Buonanno's global anti-heroines, an ambivalent and determined figure whose morality we can hardly admire. Yet she also shows support for her three future comrades, establishing a female community even in the pre-credit sequence. #MeToo style, the four women will contest female oppression across the seasons, joining forces with lesbian and transgender characters.

But there is also an in-joke for Spanish audiences in the casting here: both of the actors who play young managers in *Las chicas del cable* (Yon González and Martiño Rivas) had previously been adolescent pupils in youth mystery title *El internado* (Antena 3, 2007–10), along with the then little-known Blanca Suárez herself. While the love triangle as plot premise is familiar from US teen shows (here the characters are in their twenties), the casting is not and is a rare resource that connects only with Spaniards.

Soon the 'girls' will be clothed in their distinctive drop-waist uniforms, a turquoise counterpoint to the yellow jumpsuits in *Vis a vis*. This readily recognizable key color is another example of the instant accessibility that is built into *Las chicas del cable*, in part in an effort to attract foreign viewers. It is one that clearly worked over the long term, as shown by faithful American fans' comments on Twitter years later when the series came to an end.

Netflix's official documentary called *Money Heist: The Phenomenon* (2020) includes a lengthy sequence on the difficult shooting of a spectacular action stunt in Madrid's Plaza del Callao, on the Gran Vía, when the plot called for millions of euros to rain down on the street below from a helicopter hovering above. The documentary also shows scenes from a movie-style premiere for one of the series' seasons in the same location, which is not far from Macarena's stylish apartment building in *Vis a vis* and *Las chicas del cable*'s real-life Telefónica ('Telefonía') building.

Yet the producers and stars of the series stress throughout the documentary that it was initially a 'disaster' in Spain, canceled after the second season, and that even when it was picked up by Netflix the streamer gave it no publicity and did not anticipate its international success. The crew presents the impact of the show around the world as political (demonstrators dressed in the emblematic red overalls and Dalí masks of the characters) and even in (Álex Pina's word) 'philosophical'. Pina also repeats his assertion as to the alleged 'passion' of Latinos. But here it fits into the concept of adapting TV genres for a global audience of both sexes, which was planned from the start. *La casa de papel*, he says, combines large-scale action with intimate romance, an aspect illustrated in the documentary by a lengthy attempt to film a passionate kiss between Tokyo and her boyfriend on a Panama beach, no doubt intended as a draw for the female audience.

Interestingly, the documentary puts little stress on the USA as a market, preferring to focus on a 'giant flag' with the series' logo in Saudi Arabia and tense location shooting in Italy where crowds of fans physically endangered the newly famous cast. Yet *La casa de papel* clearly marks more fully than my previous examples a break with the Spanish market (where the series' initial 'failure' to connect with audiences is oddly celebrated) and an address to the United States as the still vital home territory of Netflix, the show's savior.

The opening episode itself is fully international in format. Its length is a swift US-standard 42 minutes and its title simply 'Episode 1' (no problems with translating tricky idioms here). And the key color, after the yellow and turquoise of my first two series, is a hot red. The first shot has Úrsula Corberó, soon to be christened Tokyo, lolling half naked on a bed under an unlikely scarlet light. The color will recur in the pre-credit sequence when her character, on the run on mean but unidentified city streets after a fatal hold up, sees a red balloon in the gray sky and is picked up by a bespectacled man in a red car. 'The Professor' will take her to the abandoned house where she will meet her comrades in the caper to come.

The gender bias skews male here: in the Professor's first class there are six men and only two women (the second is played by the Roma actor of *Vis a vis*). But the opening voice-over (as in *Las chicas del cable*) is female. And the first conversation is (as in *Vis a vis*) between a mother and a daughter who claims to be going off on a long trip. Moreover when the future Tokyo is picked up the Professor her first reaction is (as she says) to aim her pistol at his 'balls'. In spite of an apparent dose of testosterone here, then, inherited from the Anglo-Saxon heist genre, the Spanish creators highlight female action. Álex Pina was indeed the chief screenwriter for female ensemble *Vis a vis*.

Even the international angle of *La casa de papel* is to some extent undermined. As Hopewell noted, the actors speak an idiomatic Peninsular Spanish far from the 'neutral' variety once favored in exports to Latin America (lost of course in the American English dub); and if the sordid streetscapes look generic, the object of the heist, revealed some ten minutes in, is the very distinctive neo-Classical Royal Mint building in Madrid (only the facade of the historic building was used with interiors recreated in the studio). Interestingly Pina and his creative team seem to build into their unprecedented premise the broad audience address that they are seeking: the Professor tells his pupils that they must be 'popular heroes' and cannot afford to lose the public's sympathy through violence.

## Culture Heist?

In a third short promotional video Paquita Salas wanders through the open-plan offices of Netflix in Los Angeles. Where, she asks, is the boss? One employee responds helpfully in English: 'Reed Hastings? He's everywhere'. Paquita remarks slyly in Spanish that clearly he can't be bothered to come in to work.

We have seen that such stereotypes of Spanish laziness or inefficiency (which the clueless Paquita projects even on to hypermodern California) are belied by Spain's extraordinary success with streaming series for a global audience. And Netflix is well aware of the complexities of that audience. Its new 'VP of local language originals', Bela Bajaria, is a woman of Indian descent born in the UK and raised in East Africa and Los Angeles (Low 2020). She is a living reminder that the English-language community, like the Spanish, is global, and is not restricted to the United States.

A recent corporate profile in *The Economist* (2020) is skeptical about the survival of the management style that Reed Hastings is currently employing to achieve a global media giant. And it calls attention to public pressure on the 'hypermasculine' Netflix to 'care more about diversity'. Our three test cases on the platform show a trend of progressive adaptation: from the most to least female and Spanish national. There is clearly here a loss of particularity, especially for local viewers, but perhaps a gain in universality. This is Netflix's public policy, announced at the Berlin Film Festival, and it is a lesson that Spanish producers seem to have quickly learned.

We have discovered from examining the US reception of those series that an appeal to Spain and Spanish history, especially as revealed through costume and architecture, can be a competitive advantage for trade, general, and fan audiences alike, especially when combined with a female targeting that remains rarer in native US production. Spanish series can also sometimes be seen in the US as aspiring to intersectionality, as when Maureen Dowd of the *New York Times* cites Netflix's 'democratization' of media via reference to *Las chicas del cable*. Yet in so far as Spain is perceived as white and European, it is difficult to integrate its culture into American debates on diversity. The example of Álex Pina, the showrunner who shifted so swiftly from the local *Vis a vis* to the global *La casa de papel*, is vital here. It is perhaps by presenting themselves (presenting their productions) as Latinx that Spaniards will find the key to further conquering the American market, to carrying out a daring heist that is as much cultural and linguistic as it is monetary. Such a strategy may, however, cause Spanish producers to distance themselves still further from the costume dramas which made them their name at home and abroad.

## References: Text

ABOUT NETFLIX. 2020. '*Jaguar* the New Series Starring Blanca Suárez Starts Production', 7 August <https://about.netflix.com/es/news/jaguar-the-new-series-starring-blanca-suarez-starts-production> [accessed 15 September 2020]

BUCHANAN, KYLE. 2020. 'The Oscars New Diversity Rules Are Sweeping but Safe', *New York Times*, 9 September <https://www.nytimes.com/2020/09/09/movies/oscars-best-picture-diversity.html?action=click&block=more_in_recirc&impression_id=338b5140-f36b-11ea-92a9-f777707afcd2&index=0&pgtype=Article&region=footer> [accessed 15 September 2020]

—— and REGGIE UGWU. 2020. 'How the Criterion Collection Crops Out African-American Directors'. *New York Times*, 20 August <https://www.nytimes.com/interactive/2020/08/20/movies/criterion-collection-african-americans.html> [accessed 15 September 2020]

BUONANNO, MILLY. 2017. *Television Antiheroines: Women Behaving Badly in Crime and Prison Drama* (Chicago: University of Chicago Press)

——. 2014. 'Quality Television and Transnational Standards'. Lecture read at Graduate Center, CUNY, 21 November

CASCAJOSA VIRINO, CONCEPCIÓN. 2016. 'Series españolas: signos de renacimiento', *Caimán*, March, pp. 22, 24.

CORNELIO-MARÍ, ELIA MARGARITA. 2020. 'Mexican Melodrama in the Age of Netflix: Algorithms for Cultural Proximity', *Comunicación y Sociedad*, pp. 1–25 <www.comunicacionysociedad.cucsh.udg.mx/index.php/comsoc/article/view/e7481/6173> [accessed 15 September 2020]

DOWD, MAUREEN. 2020. 'Reed Hastings Had Us All Staying In Before We Had To', *New York Times*, 4 September <https://www.nytimes.com/2020/09/04/style/reed-hastings-netflix-interview.html?smid=tw-share> [accessed 15 September 2020]

*Economist, The.* 2020. 'Can Reed Hastings Preserve Netflix's Culture of Innovation As It Grows?', 12 September <https://www.economist.com/business/2020/09/12/can-reed-hastings-preserve-netflixs-culture-of-innovation-as-it-grows> [accessed 15 September 2020]

ELFRING, MAT. 2020.'Netflix Doubles Down On "Two Minute Rule" for View Counts and Explains Why', 23 January <https://www.gamespot.com/articles/netflix-doubles-down-on-two-minute-rule-for-view-c/1100-6473010/> [accessed 15 September 2020]

FRAMKE, CAROLINE. 2018. 'Netflix's Elite Subverts Teen Drama Tropes with Style', *Variety*, 23 October <https://variety.com/2018/tv/news/elite-season-1-review-netflix-1202989934/> [accessed 15 September 2020]

GEORGE, DAVID R., and WAN SONYA TANG. 2018. *Televising Restoration Spain* (Cham, Switzerland: Palgrave/Macmillan)

GLAAD. 2020. <https://www.glaad.org> [accessed 15 September 2020]

HALE, MIKE. 2019. 'The Thirty Best International TV Shows of the Decade', *New York Times*, 20 December <https://www.nytimes.com/2019/12/20/arts/television/best-international-tv-shows.html> [accessed 15 September 2020]

HOPEWELL, JOHN. 2020. 'How Netflix Grew Spain's 'Cable Girls' As It Evolved Itself', *Variety*, 3 July <https://variety.com/2020/tv/global/netflix-cable-girls-season-five-finale-1234696813/> [accessed 15 September 2020]

HOPEWELL, JOHN, and JAMIE LANG. 2019A. 'Netflix Unveils Five New Spanish Original Series', *Variety*, 6 February <https://variety.com/2019/tv/news/netflix-five-new-spanish-original-series-1203129805/> [accessed 15 September 2020]

——. 2019B. '"Money Heist" — "La casa de papel" — Creator Alex Pina: 10 Takes on Part 3'. *Variety*, 15 July <https://variety.com/2019/tv/global/money-heist-la-casa-de-papel-creator-alex-pina-10-takes-part-3-2-1203267428/#!> [accessed 15 September 2020]

'Institute on Gender and Media'. 2020. <https://seejane.org> [accessed 15 September]

LOW, ELAINE. 2020. 'Inside Netflix's Quest to Become a Global TV Giant', *Variety*, 30 July <https://variety.com/2020/tv/news/netflix-global-tv-production-bela-bajaria-1234720101/> [accessed 15 September 2020]

LYONS, MARGARET. 2017. 'How Much Watching Time Do You Have This Weekend?', *New York Times*, 4 May <https://www.nytimes.com/2017/05/04/watching/what-to-watch-weekend.html> [accessed 15 September 2020]

MARTIN, BRETT. 2013. *Difficult Men: Behind the Scenes of a Creative Revolution* (New York: Penguin)

MURRAY, NOEL. 2020. 'The Best 50 TV Shows on Netflix Now', *New York Times*, 8 September <https://www.nytimes.com/article/best-tv-shows-netflix.html> [accessed 15 September 2020]

OREN, TASHA, and SHARON SHAHAF. 2012. *Global Television Formats: Understanding Television across Borders* (Abingdon: Routledge)

OROZCO, GUILLERMO. 2020. *Televisión en tiempos de Netflix: una nueva oferta mediática* (Guadalajara: Universidad de Guadalajara) <https://drive.google.com/file/d/1quz5463cif-kuu8GqanZEgNGHal6AU9W/view?fbclid=IwAR1QOUv6g1m-vD44IRspffxa3jBWs-UiBwgReVdrXCh1b2RhvHLlIBJHmM4> [accessed 15 September 2020]

PETRI, ALEXANDRA. 2018. 'What Other Women's Stories Did You Want From CBS?' *Washington Post*, 14 September <https://www.washingtonpost.com/news/opinions/wp/2018/09/14/what-other-womens-stories-did-you-want-from-cbs/> [accessed 15 September 2020]

ROXBOROUGH, SCOTT. 2017. 'Netflix Previews European Series "Dark", "Suburra", and "Cable Girls" in Berlin', *Hollywood Reporter*, 1 March <https://www.hollywoodreporter.com/news/netflix-previews-european-series-dark-suburra-cable-girls-berlin-981888> [accessed 15 September 2020]

SMITH, PAUL JULIAN. 2019. *Multiplatform Media in Mexico: Growth and Change since 2010* (Cham, Switzerland: Palgrave/Macmillan)

## References: Audiovisual

*45 RPM*. 2019. (Bambú/Atresmedia/Netflix)

*Águila roja*. 2009–16. (Globomedia/TVE)

*Alta Mar*. 2019–20. (Bambú/Netflix)

*Casa de las Flores, La*. 2018–20. (Noc Noc Cinema/Netflix)

*casa de papel, La*. 2017–present. (Atresmedia/Netflix)

*chicas del cable, Las*. 2017–20. (Bambú/Netflix)

*Días de navidad*. 2019. (Arca/Filmax/Netflix)

*Élite*. 2018-present. (Zeta/Netflix)

*Fariña*. 2018. (Bambú/Antena 3)

*Física o química*. 2008–11. (Ida y Vuelta/Antena 3)

*Gran Hotel*. 2011–13. (Bambú/Antena 3)

*internado, El*. 2007–10. (Globomedia/Antena 3)

*Merlí*. 2015–18. (TV3 Televisió de Catalunya)

*Ministerio del Tiempo, El*. 2015–20. (Cliffhanger/RTVE)

*misterios de Laura, Los*. 2009–14. (Ida Y Vuelta/TVE)

*Mujeres asesinas*. 2008–10. (Mediamates/Televisa)

*otra mirada, La*. 2018–19. (Boomerang/RTVE)

*Paquita Salas*. 2016–present. (Flooxer/Neox/Netflix)

*Polseres vermelles*. 2011–13. (Castelao Producciones/TV3 Televisió de Catalunya)

*Tiempos de guerra.* 2017. (Bambú/Netflix)
*Valeria.* 2020. (Plano a Plano/Netflix)
*Velvet.* 2013–16. (Bambú/Antena 3/Netflix)
*Vis a vis.* 2015–19. (Globomedia/Antena 3/Netflix)

# CODA

## *Passion and Redemption: Aging in Almodóvar*

### Movies and Memories

In one scene of *Dolor y gloria* [Pain and Glory] (2019), Pedro Almodóvar's award-winning twenty-first feature film, the main character Salvador (played by Antonio Banderas), an aging, infirm, and creatively blocked filmmaker, is asked: 'How are you?' He replies quite simply with one lapidary word: 'Viejo' [Old].

What I will argue in the coda to this book, however, is that in spite of the indignities heaped on the protagonist, especially his debilitating state of health which is treated at some length in the film, age is not so absolute but is always qualified by other factors. More precisely it interacts with the three twin themes that I take to be the most important in the film: autobiography or autofiction (the latter a term much used in the field of contemporary Spanish literature); fluidity or liquidity (both literal and metaphorical); and creativity or sexuality (capacities that are shown to be closely linked in the film). The private question of individual aging in this final chapter thus supplements and intersects with the public question of collective history we have seen in the rest of the book.

While Almodóvar's attention to the theme of aging is more intense here than elsewhere, I will also argue for a retrospective perspective in which previous films anticipate this apparently novel and unexamined topic, albeit in a more discreet way. I will examine here in this light the two earlier Almodóvar films that can now be presented with *Dolor y gloria* as parts of a trilogy, one that stretches over four decades, in which the main characters are filmmakers: *La ley del deseo* [The Law of Desire] (1987) and *La mala educación* [Bad Education] (2004). I will also examine the somewhat critically neglected film that preceded *Dolor y gloria*, *Julieta* (2016). Here the focus on an aging woman, who is doubled by the younger self who is played by another actor, enables Almodóvar (and us) to address the theme of gender in its intersection with aging. Almodóvar's career famously began with the exuberant youth culture known as the *movida madrileña*. Lightly disguised and unexpected, yet invisible in plain sight, the preoccupation with aging can only now come into focus as a thread woven throughout Almodóvar's rich and varied corpus.

Let us begin, then, with *Dolor y gloria*. Here the question of autobiography (and of its relation to fiction) is both allusive and elusive. In the first place, the performance of Banderas (whose unique star profile we examined in Chapter 3) offers a near impersonation of the director's own mannerisms and the script documents physical

FIG. 7.1. Antonio Banderas as Salvador in his apartment in *Dolor y gloria*

ailments similar to those of which the auteur himself has spoken volubly in interviews. The hushed, museum-like apartment Salvador inhabits is a reproduction of the director's own, with the very same paintings hanging on the walls (we are also given its real address in the dialogue).

In spite of Almodóvar's normally guarded private life, Spanish audiences may well have been tempted to identify real-life equivalents of the figures Salvador encounters in the film: the actor he has not seen for decades and who introduces Salvador to heroin; and the lover whom he reencounters in Madrid once more, many years after their affair has ended. Salvador's central relationship with his aged mother also refers back to Almodóvar's own real-life parent, who made frequent cameos in her son's earlier films. In flashbacks, the rural poverty of the home in which the child is raised and the Catholic seminary to which he is sent are reminiscent of Almodóvar's own very frequent comments on his own upbringing in the Francoist countryside. In a self-curated special issue of cinephile magazine *Fotogramas*, the new film was re-baptized to remind faithful audiences of an old familiar title *Todo sobre mí* [All About Me]; and it was proclaimed to be the director's 'most intimate film' yet (Montano 2019). Interestingly here, for the first time and to a female journalist, Almodóvar acknowledged as welcome the influence of #MeToo and disavowed the problematic rape scenes in his earlier films.

Yet this autobiographical temptation was soon betrayed and the film's mode revealed as the more ambiguous one of autofiction. After the release of *Dolor y gloria* Almodóvar was swift to comment in interviews such as that in *Fotogramas* that, unlike his adult protagonist, he has never taken heroin; and, unlike his child protagonist, he was not raised in a cave (the authentic location here is the autonomous region of Valencia, far from Almodóvar's childhood residence of

La Mancha) (Montano 2019). In the wake of the film's shoot, the city of Paterna promoted tourism to fans eager to visit its distinctive underground homes (EFE 2019), an example of Almodóvar's ability to extend his 'home' territory beyond the familiar locations of Madrid and La Mancha.

Any supposed fixity of personal reference is thus disrupted by a pervasive fluidity and liquidity. It is telling that the film's credits play over colored streams of paint pulsing and mingling, a prelude of what is to come. The first sequence in the present is set at a swimming pool (Banderas brooding underwater cites a very similar image of an enigmatic Gael García Bernal in *La mala educación*); and the first sequence set in the past is of the mother washing laundry in a river (the child is mesmerized by running water and shimmering fish). Later Salvador's first desire will be for a workman who is naked washing himself in the family's humble home, a scene that features once more the leitmotif of water, now in a more erotic context. This sensual fluidity is also associated with cinema: at the improvised theater where Salvador sees his first films we glimpse watery shots of Marilyn Monroe and Nathalie Wood (in real life the latter would die by drowning).

Similarly, time is not linear but flows fluidly backwards and forwards. Helped by heroin, the jaded, senior Salvador re-experiences immediately and intensely the sensations first felt by himself as a child. Even the lengthy scene of conversation with the aged mother, who eagerly anticipates her own death and burial, is structured around treasured objects from Salvador's childhood, such as a darning egg. Through their persistence in time and space, such objects render past and present simultaneous, coterminous, bringing together older and younger characters or older characters with their younger selves.

The question of sex and creativity seems more problematic. The aging Salvador has suffered a loss of libido: he lives in monastic seclusion and refuses chances for new encounters with the workman who provoked his first desire (and who is linked in the film to both writing and painting) and with the lover who was his longest-lasting partner (and who is associated with the director's youthful, fruitful period during the Madrid *movida*). This sexlessness parallels his filmic block: Salvador complains throughout the film (and here of course he diverges from the ceaselessly creative Almodóvar himself) that he is unable to work, that he has no inspiration. The recovery of the workman's portrait of himself as a child does not spur Salvador on to renewed artistic productivity.

But this lament is contradicted by the film's moving and challenging final sequence. In apparent flashback, the young mother (played by Penélope Cruz) prepares to bed down with the child in a provincial railway station (a repetition of an earlier scene). The camera pulls back to reveal that we and they are in fact on a movie set and that this scene, which at first reads as a memory, is in fact a sequence that is being shot for Salvador's new film. This ending is no mere trick or sleight of hand. It proves rather that age is by no means sterile, no simple decline. To the contrary, age encompasses and recreates youth, with the first desires (for the mother, for the future male lovers) memorialized and preserved by the artistic experience to which heedless youth has no access and of which it can have no knowledge.

The film's casting can be read in a similar way. Banderas first played for Almodóvar in 1982's *Laberinto de pasiones* [Labyrinth of Passion] as an amorous young terrorist; Julieta Serrano, who is so moving as the older mother, starred in 1983's *Entre tinieblas* [Dark Habits] as a love-struck Mother Superior. As long-term spectators we register the unforgiving trace of time in the actors' bodies and on their faces (when I first saw *Dolor y gloria* in a Barcelona multiplex on its week of release the audience was overwhelmingly the mature one that would have fond memories of the earlier films when they were first shown). But we also note the cast's skill in negotiating filmic memory across lengthy careers, their sheer survival in life as in film. Banderas and Serrano serve here as actorly palimpsests, shifting fluidly once more in the public's perception, between past memory and present sensation.

## Backstories

As we gaze on the grizzled Banderas of *Dolor y gloria*, we may thus be tempted to think of his youthful beauty in *La ley del deseo*, his first starring role for Almodóvar. Once more this film was a teasing autobiography, unstably fictionalized. Although the main focus of *La ley del deseo* is on a love triangle between a thirtyish film director, here called Pablo, and his two younger lovers, as José Arroyo noted in an early article called 'A Gay Seduction', Almodóvar displaces interest in the film from gay men to the 'traditional family values' of 'hermanos', both 'brothers' and 'brother and sister' (Arroyo 1992: 44). Teasingly, the transgender sibling played by Carmen Maura is even lent a feminine form of the name of Almodóvar's own brother and faithful producer: Agustín (diminutive Tinín) here becomes Tina.

Fluidity, then, is already here at once literal and metaphorical. Perhaps the most famous scene of the film (and one which graced the cover of the first edition of my book on the cinema of Almodóvar, *Desire Unlimited* (Smith 1994)) is the one where, on a baking hot night in Madrid, the extravagant Tina begs to be hosed down by the municipal workers in the street. It is the symbol of a fluid sensuality which transcends fixed boundaries and objects. And far from land locked Madrid, and on another sultry night, Banderas' character in *La ley del deseo* (called, teasingly once more, by the actor's own name, Antonio) will murder his rival by pitching him into the black sea by a lighthouse.

More generally, subjective and representational limits are once more highly fluid. A brother becomes a sister and a father a lover (Tina's unseen incestuous parent had encouraged her gender confirmation surgery). Pablo, his sister, and her girlfriend's daughter form an improvised and flexible unit, as loving as any biological family in their communal meals. Another lengthy sequence takes place in a theater where Tina is performing Jean Cocteau's *La Voix humaine* (Almodóvar's screen version of this play which keeps the original title in translation and stars Tilda Swinton, his first film in English, was released in 2020). When Tina's lover appears in the wings, it is not clear which audience Tina is acting for or, indeed, whether she is acting at all.

It is notable that relatively youthful sex is already frustrated here: Pablo has no physical relations with his first boyfriend, Juan, for whom he displaces sex into writing (Pablo's typewriter is very prominent in several scenes). And the unpublished script, which includes passages of novelistic description, emphasizes their difference in age, claiming that Pablo leads Juan to the bedroom as one would 'a child' (Almodóvar 1987: 31). Later the older Pablo has to teach his second inexperienced boyfriend, Antonio, how to make love. There is moreover some premature attention paid to the theme of aging in the context of these affairs. The script, which I consulted in the offices of El Deseo, the production company named for this very film (Almodóvar 1987), comments on the dubious benefits of celebrity, which the filmmaker encountered at a relatively late age; and contrasts Pablo's middle-aged sluggishness on awaking in the morning with the younger Antonio's vibrant energy from the get go (Smith 1994: 79–80).

Even, then, in a film associated with the height of the *movida* youth movement, the theme of age is already present and treated with some ambivalence. Banderas' Antonio may be youthful and energetic, but he is also pathologically jealous and homicidal. His is an unstable combination of fresh-faced, athletic exuberance and psychic disturbance which Chris Perriam identified as central to the actor's masculine star profile at this time (Perriam 2003: 46–50). As the film advances, the more discreet and distanced passions of early middle age, as embodied by Pablo, seem increasingly attractive. In *Dolor y gloria*, old age, although shown in traditional style as a painful physical decline, seeks to immortalize and memorialize youth; in *La ley del deseo* middle age seeks in vain to script youth (Pablo even types himself the letters that he wishes to receive from his lover) and finally survives it (Antonio commits suicide with a gun and in the last scene is cradled, dead, in the mourning Pablo's arms).

Over a decade later the yet more complex *La mala educación* played with the autobiographical mode once more. Here the protagonist is again a filmmaker; and flashbacks, or more properly, sequences from a film within the film taking place in the past, are set in a Francoist seminary (like those later in *Dolor y gloria*). These scenes also replay in a darker and more sinister tone, the confrontation between Tina and her beloved priest teacher in a chapel in *La ley del deseo*. Released at a time when priestly abuse of children was becoming better known in the press in Spain, *La mala educación* attests in part to the tragic consequences of such abuse in its victims. But in interview on its release, Almodóvar refused to say whether he had known of abuse himself at that time in his own seminary, much less whether he himself had been abused (Smith 2014: 184–85).

Two key scenes here stress liquidity. When the protagonist filmmaker of *La mala educación* invites an aspiring actor to his home a lengthy sequence is set at a swimming pool. It is here that the young and handsome Mexican Gael García Bernal is shown, like Banderas twenty years later, brooding under water. It is clear that water is the setting for a kind of erotic spectacle for the older protagonist, from whose point of view we see. Equally fluid and much more disturbing is the scene in the same film of seminary children bathing at the idyllic river during the Francoist period. Here an objective shot of the boys sporting in the water in slow motion implicates the viewer in the voyeurism of the older characters. And this shot is juxtaposed with the (unseen) abuse of the child protagonist by a priest which takes place on the banks of the same river.

But in spite of this allusion to an urgent and pressing social issue of the time in which he made the film, Almodóvar blurs once more the fixed boundaries between reality and fiction. The child, now grown into the trans woman also played by García Bernal, threatens to blackmail the priest, oddly enough, not with autobiographical confession but with a short story based on his/her experience. Its title 'La visita' [The Visit] is one of Almodóvar's own still unpublished stories from the 1970s, before he became a filmmaker, which can be consulted in Madrid's Biblioteca Nacional, along with another story on the unlikely erotic odyssey of an elderly woman, 'El anuncio' [The Advertisement] (Almodóvar Caballero 1975; Smith 2009).

At one point in *La mala educación*, as he will do in the railway station scene in *Dolor y gloria*, Almodóvar pulls his camera back once more to reveal that the ex-student's deadly confrontation with the priest is actually a scene from the protagonist's latest film. The theme of acting is ubiquitous here (García Bernal plays no fewer than three characters of fluctuating fictional status), as is the relation between sex and creativity. More physically active, even rapacious, than the filmmaker in *La ley del deseo*, *La mala educación*'s established cineaste will pursue an affair with the younger inexperienced actor, one that he presents in voice-over with knowing cynicism as an extended 'audition'.

Once more the theme of aging is key here. The pedophilia of the first, Francoist priest (the subject of the story and film within the film titled 'La visita', played by Mexican veteran Daniel Giménez Cacho) is juxtaposed with the worn and tired flesh of the second priest (played by the equally distinguished Catalan thespian Lluís Homar), the lover of García Bernal's character in the 'real-life' portion of the plot. Most distressing to the audience and senior character is a lovemaking scene between this second mismatched couple caught on camera by the youth, as if intended to punish the older man for his undesirability, for his irremediable physical decline and improper and self-defeating desire for a much younger man.

Casting is vital here once more. The exhausted and sickened Lluís Homar, presented here as an inappropriately aged partner for the youthfully handsome but morally vicious García Bernal, will later be cast as the lover of the younger Penélope Cruz in *Los abrazos rotos* (Broken Embraces, 2009), in another example of pairing that is unequal in looks and age. Where the erotic desires of a mature man are shown as finally creative in *Dolor y gloria* (as in *La ley del deseo*), albeit sublimated into filmmaking, in *La mala educación* they can be only crippling and disabling. Homar's priest, blackmailed himself, is mortally ill and racked by an uncontrollable cough.

As I mentioned earlier, these two films can now be read from a retrospective perspective as part of a trilogy on filmmaking and filmmakers. Yet their conclusions are very different. In *La ley del deseo* the younger man, the victim of suicide, is a definitively lost love object for the mourning older man, who once thought himself to be in control of life and film. In *La mala educación*, we are told in final on-screen titles that the filmmaker continues his 'passion' for creating cinema once the relationship is finished, while the young actor is consigned to what is, for Almodóvar, the living death of work on television series. If aging might be seen, then, as maturation in creativity, that creativity is achieved (as in *Dolor y gloria*) only at the cost of solitude.

When *Julieta* was released in 2016, just three years before *Dolor y gloria*, it passed almost unnoticed by critics and audiences, its affluent cloistered characters and abstract milieu out of sympathy with a Spain still reeling from the financial crisis. Yet in its premise of an older woman juxtaposed throughout with her younger self and played by two different actors, *Julieta* also provides a subtle reflection on the theme of aging, this time from a female perspective. Casting is vital here again. The older Emma Suárez is best remembered by international art-house audiences for youthful roles for Julio Medem, where she often played parts younger than her actual age (her character begins *Vacas* (1992) as a child, although the actor was approaching thirty). Adriana Ugarte, who plays the young Julieta, does not benefit from Suárez's artistic halo or cinematic palimpsest, as she is best known to Spanish viewers for her starring roles in period miniseries on television, that medium so despised by Almodóvar.

*Julieta*'s feminine register tends to obviate questions of autobiography or autofiction, even given the possibilities for cross-gender identification offered elsewhere by Almodóvar (we remember how in *La ley del deseo* he transformed his brother Agustín into his character trans-woman Tina). *Julieta* begins with a shot of billowing red fabric whose folds are reminiscent of a vagina (featured also on the film's poster, it proves to be the older protagonist's bathrobe). And its female protagonist is no filmmaker or creator. Originally an ancient history lecturer at the university (a profession and setting that could hardly be further from those of the autodidact cineaste Almodóvar), Julieta later settles for odd jobs in copy-editing. It is significant that although half of the film is set in the 1980s we see no sign of the vibrant youth culture of the period with which Almodóvar remains so associated. Artistic creation, its delights and discontents, are displaced here into maternity, a preoccupation that does not wane with age. Julieta's constant concern as an older woman is for the daughter who has inexplicably abandoned her.

The plotting here, except for its crosscutting between past and present, is much less fluid than in Almodóvar's other films. Indeed much of the running time feels, like Julieta herself, static: suspended in mourning and melancholia by the lost object that is the daughter. The pace of the action is also much slower, more deliberate, than in the earlier titles with their more complex plotting and swifter cutting. Tellingly, liquid is also absent. Indeed, characteristically, Almodóvar himself described his film as in Spanish as 'seco' [dry] (Smith 2016: 65). Julieta retires to an arid Madrid that is no longer, in the words of Marvin D'Lugo, the youthful 'city of desire' of Almodóvar's early films (D'Lugo 1991), after the loss of the daughter; and that daughter abandons the mother in the stark green mountains of Aragón. The main erotic scene in the film is set in a train where the young Julieta makes love with her future husband as they traverse the countryside. Inexplicably they are joined by a deer that runs alongside the vehicle, the apparent animal spirit of that rural place. This, then, is a film of the land.

The one liquid location is the ocean off Galicia where Julieta lives briefly with her unlikely husband who proves to be a fisherman. It is an ominous and cold northern seascape in which the husband meets his death and which could not be further from the joyous spurt of water that arcs across the hot night sky in *La ley del deseo* to flood an ecstatic Tina. And the older Julieta, like Salvador in *Dolor y gloria*, is chaste. Comparable also to another of Almodóvar's mourning parents, Cecilia Roth in *Todo sobre mi madre* [All About My Mother] (1999), Julieta is condemned compulsively to repeat the loss of her perfect child, for whom no love object can substitute.

This replacement of sexuality and artistic creativity by maternity in a feminine key is of course problematic. Must it always be the case that the aging woman has no sex life? And even if we redefine sexuality as an eroticism that goes beyond genital coupling (as it does in the liquid sensuality of the scenes I have mentioned above in *Dolor y gloria*, *La ley del deseo* and *La mala educación*), *Julieta* offers no similar moments of abstracted sensuous abandon to its abstemious or depressed heroine.

The lost (male) lovers of the other three films, Almodóvar's trilogy of filmmakers, are here replaced by a lost daughter, whose motivation for abandoning the parent who loves her remains obscure. This is unlike the beloved men elsewhere, who have their reasons, however ambivalent or even sinister, for taking their leave: the murderous Antonio in *La ley del deseo* commits suicide after one perfect night of love; the treacherous Ángel or Juan (he uses both names) in *La mala educación* abandons the older priest and the film director who have supported him; Santiago's Argentine lover Federico in *Dolor y gloria* flees back to Buenos Aires to escape the trap of drug addiction in Madrid.

In a kind of abrupt and unmotivated *deus ex machina*, Almodóvar provides us in *Julieta* with a final but unreliable resolution: after many years Julieta receives a letter from her daughter, now herself a mother, apologizing for her absence and seeking reconciliation with her. But the climactic scene itself is unshown, appears to be unrepresentable, and the film ends with Julieta still traveling on the road. The role of the older woman, then, seems to be to experience an inexplicable loss and an invisible restitution. This is a process which, unlike in the other films which focused on men, is not compensated for by the intense redemptive pleasures of creativity, however solitary they may be. The old age of a woman would thus appear to have no advantages. Julieta is not even comforted by the ecstatic and erotic memories of childhood (the so-called 'first desire') which the troubled Salvador enjoys and transforms into his filmic art. She can only be whole when reunited with her daughter.

*Dolor y gloria* stresses somewhat relentlessly the indignities of male aging. Primarily these indignities are physical, albeit rendered visually attractive by Juan Gatti's elegant animated anatomical sequences or Banderas' subtly moving performance. But Salvador is also psychically diminished by age, rendered indifferent to the needs of others, trapped as he is in the ailing body that obsesses him and prevents him from reaching out to others. Not always sympathetic, he treats his female assistant with an especial lack of concern that is made clearly visible to the audience. Yet the trilogy as a whole shows that salvation and reclamation can be achieved, for older men at least, through art: in spite of the complaints and fears of the aptly named Salvador [Savior], his and Almodóvar's creativity remains undimmed.

Moreover, and here is the key point, while the older woman is bereft without her child, the older childless man (Salvador, Almodóvar, once more) can still incorporate maternity into his own final narrative. In the last scene of *Dolor y gloria*, mother and child are shown tenderly settling down to sleep in the film within the film. But this scene only takes place under the direction of the filmmaker who stays in a privileged position off set and is revealed when the camera pulls back and the actors break character within the film that we are witnessing. The final moral would seem to be that for Almodóvar age may in traditional style disable the body, a temporal process we have seen in all four films we have examined. But psychic maturity can still transcend physical deterioration, at least for those fortunate older men for whom filmmaking remains a continuing passion and a redemption from unremitting decline.

## Period Pieces and Places of Memory

It is perhaps not unexpected that the most representative of Spanish audiovisual creators should have something in common with the subjects of all of the past chapters in this book. Thus we saw that for the Javis Almodóvar serves as a crucial reference to the cinematic past that is recreated in their own multimedia fictions; and that he can also be seen as a middle term in a 'homosexual genealogy' which stretches back from the young contemporary couple to the García Lorca whose rural tragedy they remade in a special episode of *Paquita Salas*.

Likewise *Dolor y gloria*, as a very explicit example of autofiction, serves as a kind of a period piece or bio-pic of its own creator, even if its somewhat ironic tone allies Almodóvar's film more with the skeptical version of Picasso and his work that we saw in TVE's *El Ministerio del Tiempo* than with the hagiographic vision of National Geographic's *Genius*. And like the producers of that lost genre of the classic serial, Almodóvar can be seen here as engaging in a kind of historical pedagogy, educating his faithful but perhaps forgetful aging audience on now distant periods that remain within (his and their) living memory: the repressive sixties and hedonistic eighties, which contrast with the hard won realism of a present in physical, if not artistic, decline.

Finally, although not so much in *Dolor y gloria*, Almodóvar has chronicled his Spain through fragile female characters who are as touching and moving as the maid in *Arde Madrid* (for example, Tina in *La ley del deseo*) and through improvised female communities as loving and conflicted as that of the teachers and schoolgirls in *La otra mirada* (for example, the convent in *Entre tinieblas*). And, with some forty years of international success behind him, he is a unique industrial precedent for the current global vogue for Spanish series, also female-focused, that we have seen on Netflix.

Yet, in a visual culture context, perhaps the closest connection between this coda and the earlier chapters is in the uncanny survival of an unexpected medium: painting. As we just saw, *Dolor y gloria*'s plot and psychological development explicitly turns on a modest watercolor portrait as continuing testimony to a decisive 'first desire'; and the film implicitly uses its directors own collection of now period Spanish paintings (by *movida* luminaries such as Guillermo Pérez Villalta) to chart the history of its subject and his city.

Of course in the two texts I studied, Picasso's *Guernica* serves as a unique example of a peripatetic masterpiece, reflecting and refracting the nation even as it stays outside it. But in the chapter on Lorca we also saw that the Ministry of Time's mission is prompted by an anomalous and anachronistic art work (an early Dalí picture that includes an iPad); and in a chapter on gender we saw how the credits to *La otra mirada* show a paintbrush fashioning a new kind of woman's eyes, a new artistic look at that woman (in painterly styles from Impressionist to Cubist). Even the fetishistic emphasis on the decorative or applied arts in costume drama (love seats in *Fortunata y Jacinta*; cloche hats and drop-waist dresses in *Las chicas del cable*) testifies to historical material objects both as charged places of memory and as potent sources of pleasure for contemporary audiences. It is through such varied but linked techniques that contemporary Spanish audiovisual creators have so deftly reimagined their history.

## References: Text

ALMODÓVAR, PEDRO. 1987. 'La ley del deseo: guión' (Madrid), unpublished typescript held in the offices of El Deseo

ALMODÓVAR CABALLERO, PEDRO. 1975. 'Relatos' (Madrid), unpublished typescript held in the Biblioteca Nacional

ARROYO, JOSÉ. 1992. '*La ley del deseo*: A Gay Seduction', in *European Popular Cinema*, ed. by Richard Dyer and Ginette Vincendeau (New York and London: Routledge), pp. 31–46

D'LUGO, MARVIN. 1991. 'Almodóvar's City of Desire', *Quarterly Review of Film and Video*, 13.4: 47–65

EFE. 2019. 'Ruta por "las cuevas de Almodóvar" en Paterna', *La Vanguardia*, 24 April <https://www.lavanguardia.com/ocio/viajes/20190424/461707763683/paterna-pelicula-almodovar-dolor-y-gloria-ruta.html> [accessed 24 February 2021]

MONTANO, ALICIA G. 2019. 'Pedro Almodóvar nos habla de *Dolor y gloria*, su película más íntima', *Fotogramas*, 22 March <https://www.fotogramas.es/noticias-cine/a26905764/dolor-y-gloria-pedro-almodovar-entrevista/> [accessed 24 February 2021]

PERRIAM, CHRIS. 2003. *Stars and Masculinities in Spanish Cinema: Banderas to Bardem* (Oxford and New York: Oxford University Press)

SMITH, PAUL JULIAN. 1994. *Desire Unlimited: The Cinema of Pedro Almodóvar*, 1st edn (London and New York: Verso)

——. 2009. 'Almodóvar's Unpublished Short Stories and the Question of Queer Auteurism', *Screen*, 50.4: 439–49

——. 2014. *Desire Unlimited: The Cinema of Pedro Almodóvar*, 2nd edn (London and New York: Verso)

——. 2016. 'Letter from Madrid: Spanish Screenings and *Julieta*', *Film Quarterly*, 70.2: 63–67

## References: Audiovisual

*Laberinto de pasiones*. 1982. Dir. by Pedro Almodóvar (El Deseo)

*Entre tinieblas*. 1983. Dir. by Pedro Almodóvar (El Deseo)

*ley del deseo, La.* 1987. Dir. by Pedro Almodóvar (El Deseo)
*Todo sobre mi madre.* 1999. Dir. by Pedro Almodóvar (El Deseo)
*mala educación, La.* 2004. Dir. by Pedro Almodóvar (El Deseo)
*Volver.* 2006. Dir. by Pedro Almodóvar (El Deseo)
*Julieta.* 2016. Dir. by Pedro Almodóvar (El Deseo)
*Dolor y gloria.* 2019. Dir. by Pedro Almodóvar (El Deseo)
*The Human Voice.* 2020. Dir. by Pedro Almodóvar (El Deseo)

# INDEX

Milton Keynes UK
Ingram Content Group UK Ltd.
UKHW050325180924
448405UK00008B/66